Mometrix
TEST PREPARATION

LEP®

ntroduction to Educational sychology Exam

ecrets Study Guide

DEAR FUTURE EXAM SUCCESS STORY

First of all, **THANK YOU** for purchasing Mometrix study materials!

Second, congratulations! You are one of the few determined test-takers who are committed to doing whatever it takes to excel on your exam. **You have come to the right place.** We developed these study materials with one goal in mind: to deliver you the information you need in a format that's concise and easy to use.

In addition to optimizing your guide for the content of the test, we've outlined our recommended steps for breaking down the preparation process into small, attainable goals so you can make sure you stay on track.

We've also analyzed the entire test-taking process, identifying the most common pitfalls and showing how you can overcome them and be ready for any curveball the test throws you.

Standardized testing is one of the biggest obstacles on your road to success, which only increases the importance of doing well in the high-pressure, high-stakes environment of test day. Your results on this test could have a significant impact on your future, and this guide provides the information and practical advice to help you achieve your full potential on test day.

Your success is our success

We would love to hear from you! If you would like to share the story of your exam success or if you have any questions or comments in regard to our products, please contact us at **800-673-8175** or **support@mometrix.com**.

Thanks again for your business and we wish you continued success!

Sincerely,
The Mometrix Test Preparation Team

Need more help? Check out our flashcards at:
http://MometrixFlashcards.com/CLEP

Written and edited by the Mometrix Exam Secrets Test Prep Team
Printed in the United States of America

TABLE OF CONTENTS

Introduction

Thank you for purchasing this resource! You have made the choice to prepare yourself for a test that could have a huge impact on your future, and this guide is designed to help you be fully ready for test day. Obviously, it's important to have a solid understanding of the test material, but you also need to be prepared for the unique environment and stressors of the test, so that you can perform to the best of your abilities.

For this purpose, the first section that appears in this guide is the **Secret Keys**. We've devoted countless hours to meticulously researching what works and what doesn't, and we've boiled down our findings to the five most impactful steps you can take to improve your performance on the test. We start at the beginning with study planning and move through the preparation process, all the way to the testing strategies that will help you get the most out of what you know when you're finally sitting in front of the test.

We recommend that you start preparing for your test as far in advance as possible. However, if you've bought this guide as a last-minute study resource and only have a few days before your test, we recommend that you skip over the first two Secret Keys since they address a long-term study plan.

If you struggle with **test anxiety**, we strongly encourage you to check out our recommendations for how you can overcome it. Test anxiety is a formidable foe, but it can be beaten, and we want to make sure you have the tools you need to defeat it.

Secret Key #1 – Plan Big, Study Small

There's a lot riding on your performance. If you want to ace this test, you're going to need to keep your skills sharp and the material fresh in your mind. You need a plan that lets you review everything you need to know while still fitting in your schedule. We'll break this strategy down into three categories.

Information Organization

Start with the information you already have: the official test outline. From this, you can make a complete list of all the concepts you need to cover before the test. Organize these concepts into groups that can be studied together, and create a list of any related vocabulary you need to learn so you can brush up on any difficult terms. You'll want to keep this vocabulary list handy once you actually start studying since you may need to add to it along the way.

Time Management

Once you have your set of study concepts, decide how to spread them out over the time you have left before the test. Break your study plan into small, clear goals so you have a manageable task for each day and know exactly what you're doing. Then just focus on one small step at a time. When you manage your time this way, you don't need to spend hours at a time studying. Studying a small block of content for a short period each day helps you retain information better and avoid stressing over how much you have left to do. You can relax knowing that you have a plan to cover everything in time. In order for this strategy to be effective though, you have to start studying early and stick to your schedule. Avoid the exhaustion and futility that comes from last-minute cramming!

Study Environment

The environment you study in has a big impact on your learning. Studying in a coffee shop, while probably more enjoyable, is not likely to be as fruitful as studying in a quiet room. It's important to keep distractions to a minimum. You're only planning to study for a short block of time, so make the most of it. Don't pause to check your phone or get up to find a snack. It's also important to **avoid multitasking**. Research has consistently shown that multitasking will make your studying dramatically less effective. Your study area should also be comfortable and well-lit so you don't have the distraction of straining your eyes or sitting on an uncomfortable chair.

The time of day you study is also important. You want to be rested and alert. Don't wait until just before bedtime. Study when you'll be most likely to comprehend and remember. Even better, if you know what time of day your test will be, set that time aside for study. That way your brain will be used to working on that subject at that specific time and you'll have a better chance of recalling information.

Finally, it can be helpful to team up with others who are studying for the same test. Your actual studying should be done in as isolated an environment as possible, but the work of organizing the information and setting up the study plan can be divided up. In between study sessions, you can discuss with your teammates the concepts that you're all studying and quiz each other on the details. Just be sure that your teammates are as serious about the test as you are. If you find that your study time is being replaced with social time, you might need to find a new team.

Secret Key #2 – Make Your Studying Count

You're devoting a lot of time and effort to preparing for this test, so you want to be absolutely certain it will pay off. This means doing more than just reading the content and hoping you can remember it on test day. It's important to make every minute of study count. There are two main areas you can focus on to make your studying count.

Retention

It doesn't matter how much time you study if you can't remember the material. You need to make sure you are retaining the concepts. To check your retention of the information you're learning, try recalling it at later times with minimal prompting. Try carrying around flashcards and glance at one or two from time to time or ask a friend who's also studying for the test to quiz you.

To enhance your retention, look for ways to put the information into practice so that you can apply it rather than simply recalling it. If you're using the information in practical ways, it will be much easier to remember. Similarly, it helps to solidify a concept in your mind if you're not only reading it to yourself but also explaining it to someone else. Ask a friend to let you teach them about a concept you're a little shaky on (or speak aloud to an imaginary audience if necessary). As you try to summarize, define, give examples, and answer your friend's questions, you'll understand the concepts better and they will stay with you longer. Finally, step back for a big picture view and ask yourself how each piece of information fits with the whole subject. When you link the different concepts together and see them working together as a whole, it's easier to remember the individual components.

Finally, practice showing your work on any multi-step problems, even if you're just studying. Writing out each step you take to solve a problem will help solidify the process in your mind, and you'll be more likely to remember it during the test.

Modality

Modality simply refers to the means or method by which you study. Choosing a study modality that fits your own individual learning style is crucial. No two people learn best in exactly the same way, so it's important to know your strengths and use them to your advantage.

For example, if you learn best by visualization, focus on visualizing a concept in your mind and draw an image or a diagram. Try color-coding your notes, illustrating them, or creating symbols that will trigger your mind to recall a learned concept. If you learn best by hearing or discussing information, find a study partner who learns the same way or read aloud to yourself. Think about how to put the information in your own words. Imagine that you are giving a lecture on the topic and record yourself so you can listen to it later.

For any learning style, flashcards can be helpful. Organize the information so you can take advantage of spare moments to review. Underline key words or phrases. Use different colors for different categories. Mnemonic devices (such as creating a short list in which every item starts with the same letter) can also help with retention. Find what works best for you and use it to store the information in your mind most effectively and easily.

Secret Key #3 – Practice the Right Way

Your success on test day depends not only on how many hours you put into preparing, but also on whether you prepared the right way. It's good to check along the way to see if your studying is paying off. One of the most effective ways to do this is by taking practice tests to evaluate your progress. Practice tests are useful because they show exactly where you need to improve. Every time you take a practice test, pay special attention to these three groups of questions:

- The questions you got wrong
- The questions you had to guess on, even if you guessed right
- The questions you found difficult or slow to work through

This will show you exactly what your weak areas are, and where you need to devote more study time. Ask yourself why each of these questions gave you trouble. Was it because you didn't understand the material? Was it because you didn't remember the vocabulary? Do you need more repetitions on this type of question to build speed and confidence? Dig into those questions and figure out how you can strengthen your weak areas as you go back to review the material.

Additionally, many practice tests have a section explaining the answer choices. It can be tempting to read the explanation and think that you now have a good understanding of the concept. However, an explanation likely only covers part of the question's broader context. Even if the explanation makes perfect sense, **go back and investigate** every concept related to the question until you're positive you have a thorough understanding.

As you go along, keep in mind that the practice test is just that: practice. Memorizing these questions and answers will not be very helpful on the actual test because it is unlikely to have any of the same exact questions. If you only know the right answers to the sample questions, you won't be prepared for the real thing. **Study the concepts** until you understand them fully, and then you'll be able to answer any question that shows up on the test.

It's important to wait on the practice tests until you're ready. If you take a test on your first day of study, you may be overwhelmed by the amount of material covered and how much you need to learn. Work up to it gradually.

On test day, you'll need to be prepared for answering questions, managing your time, and using the test-taking strategies you've learned. It's a lot to balance, like a mental marathon that will have a big impact on your future. Like training for a marathon, you'll need to start slowly and work your way up. When test day arrives, you'll be ready.

Start with the strategies you've read in the first two Secret Keys—plan your course and study in the way that works best for you. If you have time, consider using multiple study resources to get different approaches to the same concepts. It can be helpful to see difficult concepts from more than one angle. Then find a good source for practice tests. Many times, the test website will suggest potential study resources or provide sample tests.

Practice Test Strategy

If you're able to find at least three practice tests, we recommend this strategy:

Untimed and Open-Book Practice

Take the first test with no time constraints and with your notes and study guide handy. Take your time and focus on applying the strategies you've learned.

Timed and Open-Book Practice

Take the second practice test open-book as well, but set a timer and practice pacing yourself to finish in time.

Timed and Closed-Book Practice

Take any other practice tests as if it were test day. Set a timer and put away your study materials. Sit at a table or desk in a quiet room, imagine yourself at the testing center, and answer questions as quickly and accurately as possible.

Keep repeating timed and closed-book tests on a regular basis until you run out of practice tests or it's time for the actual test. Your mind will be ready for the schedule and stress of test day, and you'll be able to focus on recalling the material you've learned.

Secret Key #4 – Pace Yourself

Once you're fully prepared for the material on the test, your biggest challenge on test day will be managing your time. Just knowing that the clock is ticking can make you panic even if you have plenty of time left. Work on pacing yourself so you can build confidence against the time constraints of the exam. Pacing is a difficult skill to master, especially in a high-pressure environment, so **practice is vital**.

Set time expectations for your pace based on how much time is available. For example, if a section has 60 questions and the time limit is 30 minutes, you know you have to average 30 seconds or less per question in order to answer them all. Although 30 seconds is the hard limit, set 25 seconds per question as your goal, so you reserve extra time to spend on harder questions. When you budget extra time for the harder questions, you no longer have any reason to stress when those questions take longer to answer.

Don't let this time expectation distract you from working through the test at a calm, steady pace, but keep it in mind so you don't spend too much time on any one question. Recognize that taking extra time on one question you don't understand may keep you from answering two that you do understand later in the test. If your time limit for a question is up and you're still not sure of the answer, mark it and move on, and come back to it later if the time and the test format allow. If the testing format doesn't allow you to return to earlier questions, just make an educated guess; then put it out of your mind and move on.

On the easier questions, be careful not to rush. It may seem wise to hurry through them so you have more time for the challenging ones, but it's not worth missing one if you know the concept and just didn't take the time to read the question fully. Work efficiently but make sure you understand the question and have looked at all of the answer choices, since more than one may seem right at first.

Even if you're paying attention to the time, you may find yourself a little behind at some point. You should speed up to get back on track, but do so wisely. Don't panic; just take a few seconds less on each question until you're caught up. Don't guess without thinking, but do look through the answer choices and eliminate any you know are wrong. If you can get down to two choices, it is often worthwhile to guess from those. Once you've chosen an answer, move on and don't dwell on any that you skipped or had to hurry through. If a question was taking too long, chances are it was one of the harder ones, so you weren't as likely to get it right anyway.

On the other hand, if you find yourself getting ahead of schedule, it may be beneficial to slow down a little. The more quickly you work, the more likely you are to make a careless mistake that will affect your score. You've budgeted time for each question, so don't be afraid to spend that time. Practice an efficient but careful pace to get the most out of the time you have.

Secret Key #5 – Have a Plan for Guessing

When you're taking the test, you may find yourself stuck on a question. Some of the answer choices seem better than others, but you don't see the one answer choice that is obviously correct. What do you do?

The scenario described above is very common, yet most test takers have not effectively prepared for it. Developing and practicing a plan for guessing may be one of the single most effective uses of your time as you get ready for the exam.

In developing your plan for guessing, there are three questions to address:

- When should you start the guessing process?
- How should you narrow down the choices?
- Which answer should you choose?

When to Start the Guessing Process

Unless your plan for guessing is to select C every time (which, despite its merits, is not what we recommend), you need to leave yourself enough time to apply your answer elimination strategies. Since you have a limited amount of time for each question, that means that if you're going to give yourself the best shot at guessing correctly, you have to decide quickly whether or not you will guess.

Of course, the best-case scenario is that you don't have to guess at all, so first, see if you can answer the question based on your knowledge of the subject and basic reasoning skills. Focus on the key words in the question and try to jog your memory of related topics. Give yourself a chance to bring the knowledge to mind, but once you realize that you don't have (or you can't access) the knowledge you need to answer the question, it's time to start the guessing process.

It's almost always better to start the guessing process too early than too late. It only takes a few seconds to remember something and answer the question from knowledge. Carefully eliminating wrong answer choices takes longer. Plus, going through the process of eliminating answer choices can actually help jog your memory.

Summary: Start the guessing process as soon as you decide that you can't answer the question based on your knowledge.

How to Narrow Down the Choices

The next chapter in this book (**Test-Taking Strategies**) includes a wide range of strategies for how to approach questions and how to look for answer choices to eliminate. You will definitely want to read those carefully, practice them, and figure out which ones work best for you. Here though, we're going to address a mindset rather than a particular strategy.

Your odds of guessing an answer correctly depend on how many options you are choosing from.

Number of options left	5	4	3	2	1
Odds of guessing correctly	20%	25%	33%	50%	100%

You can see from this chart just how valuable it is to be able to eliminate incorrect answers and make an educated guess, but there are two things that many test takers do that cause them to miss out on the benefits of guessing:

- Accidentally eliminating the correct answer
- Selecting an answer based on an impression

We'll look at the first one here, and the second one in the next section.

To avoid accidentally eliminating the correct answer, we recommend a thought exercise called **the $5 challenge**. In this challenge, you only eliminate an answer choice from contention if you are willing to bet $5 on it being wrong. Why $5? Five dollars is a small but not insignificant amount of money. It's an amount you could afford to lose but wouldn't want to throw away. And while losing $5 once might not hurt too much, doing it twenty times will set you back $100. In the same way, each small decision you make—eliminating a choice here, guessing on a question there—won't by itself impact your score very much, but when you put them all together, they can make a big difference. By holding each answer choice elimination decision to a higher standard, you can reduce the risk of accidentally eliminating the correct answer.

The $5 challenge can also be applied in a positive sense: If you are willing to bet $5 that an answer choice *is* correct, go ahead and mark it as correct.

Summary: Only eliminate an answer choice if you are willing to bet $5 that it is wrong.

Which Answer to Choose

You're taking the test. You've run into a hard question and decided you'll have to guess. You've eliminated all the answer choices you're willing to bet $5 on. Now you have to pick an answer. Why do we even need to talk about this? Why can't you just pick whichever one you feel like when the time comes?

The answer to these questions is that if you don't come into the test with a plan, you'll rely on your impression to select an answer choice, and if you do that, you risk falling into a trap. The test writers know that everyone who takes their test will be guessing on some of the questions, so they intentionally write wrong answer choices to seem plausible. You still have to pick an answer though, and if the wrong answer choices are designed to look right, how can you ever be sure that you're not falling for their trap? The best solution we've found to this dilemma is to take the decision out of your hands entirely. Here is the process we recommend:

Once you've eliminated any choices that you are confident (willing to bet $5) are wrong, select the first remaining choice as your answer.

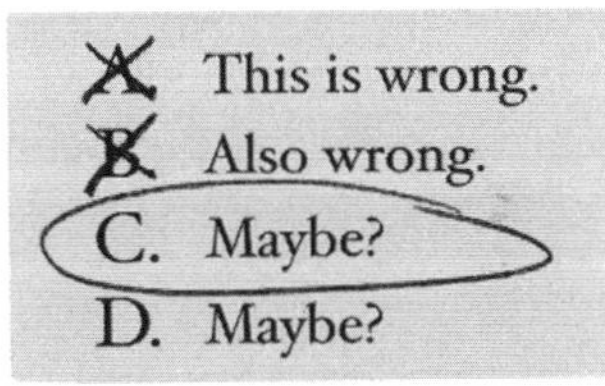

Whether you choose to select the first remaining choice, the second, or the last, the important thing is that you use some preselected standard. Using this approach guarantees that you will not be enticed into selecting an answer choice that looks right, because you are not basing your decision on how the answer choices look.

This is not meant to make you question your knowledge. Instead, it is to help you recognize the difference between your knowledge and your impressions. There's a huge difference between thinking an answer is right because of what you know, and thinking an answer is right because it looks or sounds like it should be right.

Summary: To ensure that your selection is appropriately random, make a predetermined selection from among all answer choices you have not eliminated.

Test-Taking Strategies

This section contains a list of test-taking strategies that you may find helpful as you work through the test. By taking what you know and applying logical thought, you can maximize your chances of answering any question correctly!

It is very important to realize that every question is different and every person is different: no single strategy will work on every question, and no single strategy will work for every person. That's why we've included all of them here, so you can try them out and determine which ones work best for different types of questions and which ones work best for you.

Question Strategies

⊘ Read Carefully

Read the question and the answer choices carefully. Don't miss the question because you misread the terms. You have plenty of time to read each question thoroughly and make sure you understand what is being asked. Yet a happy medium must be attained, so don't waste too much time. You must read carefully and efficiently.

⊘ Contextual Clues

Look for contextual clues. If the question includes a word you are not familiar with, look at the immediate context for some indication of what the word might mean. Contextual clues can often give you all the information you need to decipher the meaning of an unfamiliar word. Even if you can't determine the meaning, you may be able to narrow down the possibilities enough to make a solid guess at the answer to the question.

⊘ Prefixes

If you're having trouble with a word in the question or answer choices, try dissecting it. Take advantage of every clue that the word might include. Prefixes can be a huge help. Usually, they allow you to determine a basic meaning. *Pre-* means before, *post-* means after, *pro-* is positive, *de-* is negative. From prefixes, you can get an idea of the general meaning of the word and try to put it into context.

⊘ Hedge Words

Watch out for critical hedge words, such as *likely, may, can, often, almost, mostly, usually, generally, rarely*, and *sometimes*. Question writers insert these hedge phrases to cover every possibility. Often an answer choice will be wrong simply because it leaves no room for exception. Be on guard for answer choices that have definitive words such as *exactly* and *always*.

⊘ Switchback Words

Stay alert for *switchbacks*. These are the words and phrases frequently used to alert you to shifts in thought. The most common switchback words are *but, although*, and *however*. Others include *nevertheless, on the other hand, even though, while, in spite of, despite*, and *regardless of*. Switchback words are important to catch because they can change the direction of the question or an answer choice.

✓ Face Value

When in doubt, use common sense. Accept the situation in the problem at face value. Don't read too much into it. These problems will not require you to make wild assumptions. If you have to go beyond creativity and warp time or space in order to have an answer choice fit the question, then you should move on and consider the other answer choices. These are normal problems rooted in reality. The applicable relationship or explanation may not be readily apparent, but it is there for you to figure out. Use your common sense to interpret anything that isn't clear.

Answer Choice Strategies

✓ Answer Selection

The most thorough way to pick an answer choice is to identify and eliminate wrong answers until only one is left, then confirm it is the correct answer. Sometimes an answer choice may immediately seem right, but be careful. The test writers will usually put more than one reasonable answer choice on each question, so take a second to read all of them and make sure that the other choices are not equally obvious. As long as you have time left, it is better to read every answer choice than to pick the first one that looks right without checking the others.

✓ Answer Choice Families

An answer choice family consists of two (in rare cases, three) answer choices that are very similar in construction and cannot all be true at the same time. If you see two answer choices that are direct opposites or parallels, one of them is usually the correct answer. For instance, if one answer choice says that quantity *x* increases and another either says that quantity *x* decreases (opposite) or says that quantity *y* increases (parallel), then those answer choices would fall into the same family. An answer choice that doesn't match the construction of the answer choice family is more likely to be incorrect. Most questions will not have answer choice families, but when they do appear, you should be prepared to recognize them.

✓ Eliminate Answers

Eliminate answer choices as soon as you realize they are wrong, but make sure you consider all possibilities. If you are eliminating answer choices and realize that the last one you are left with is also wrong, don't panic. Start over and consider each choice again. There may be something you missed the first time that you will realize on the second pass.

✓ Avoid Fact Traps

Don't be distracted by an answer choice that is factually true but doesn't answer the question. You are looking for the choice that answers the question. Stay focused on what the question is asking for so you don't accidentally pick an answer that is true but incorrect. Always go back to the question and make sure the answer choice you've selected actually answers the question and is not merely a true statement.

✓ Extreme Statements

In general, you should avoid answers that put forth extreme actions as standard practice or proclaim controversial ideas as established fact. An answer choice that states the "process should be used in certain situations, if..." is much more likely to be correct than one that states the "process should be discontinued completely." The first is a calm rational statement and doesn't even make a definitive, uncompromising stance, using a hedge word *if* to provide wiggle room, whereas the second choice is far more extreme.

⊘ Benchmark

As you read through the answer choices and you come across one that seems to answer the question well, mentally select that answer choice. This is not your final answer, but it's the one that will help you evaluate the other answer choices. The one that you selected is your benchmark or standard for judging each of the other answer choices. Every other answer choice must be compared to your benchmark. That choice is correct until proven otherwise by another answer choice beating it. If you find a better answer, then that one becomes your new benchmark. Once you've decided that no other choice answers the question as well as your benchmark, you have your final answer.

⊘ Predict the Answer

Before you even start looking at the answer choices, it is often best to try to predict the answer. When you come up with the answer on your own, it is easier to avoid distractions and traps because you will know exactly what to look for. The right answer choice is unlikely to be word-for-word what you came up with, but it should be a close match. Even if you are confident that you have the right answer, you should still take the time to read each option before moving on.

General Strategies

⊘ Tough Questions

If you are stumped on a problem or it appears too hard or too difficult, don't waste time. Move on! Remember though, if you can quickly check for obviously incorrect answer choices, your chances of guessing correctly are greatly improved. Before you completely give up, at least try to knock out a couple of possible answers. Eliminate what you can and then guess at the remaining answer choices before moving on.

⊘ Check Your Work

Since you will probably not know every term listed and the answer to every question, it is important that you get credit for the ones that you do know. Don't miss any questions through careless mistakes. If at all possible, try to take a second to look back over your answer selection and make sure you've selected the correct answer choice and haven't made a costly careless mistake (such as marking an answer choice that you didn't mean to mark). This quick double check should more than pay for itself in caught mistakes for the time it costs.

⊘ Pace Yourself

It's easy to be overwhelmed when you're looking at a page full of questions; your mind is confused and full of random thoughts, and the clock is ticking down faster than you would like. Calm down and maintain the pace that you have set for yourself. Especially as you get down to the last few minutes of the test, don't let the small numbers on the clock make you panic. As long as you are on track by monitoring your pace, you are guaranteed to have time for each question.

⊘ Don't Rush

It is very easy to make errors when you are in a hurry. Maintaining a fast pace in answering questions is pointless if it makes you miss questions that you would have gotten right otherwise. Test writers like to include distracting information and wrong answers that seem right. Taking a little extra time to avoid careless mistakes can make all the difference in your test score. Find a pace that allows you to be confident in the answers that you select.

⊘ KEEP MOVING

Panicking will not help you pass the test, so do your best to stay calm and keep moving. Taking deep breaths and going through the answer elimination steps you practiced can help to break through a stress barrier and keep your pace.

Final Notes

The combination of a solid foundation of content knowledge and the confidence that comes from practicing your plan for applying that knowledge is the key to maximizing your performance on test day. As your foundation of content knowledge is built up and strengthened, you'll find that the strategies included in this chapter become more and more effective in helping you quickly sift through the distractions and traps of the test to isolate the correct answer.

Now that you're preparing to move forward into the test content chapters of this book, be sure to keep your goal in mind. As you read, think about how you will be able to apply this information on the test. If you've already seen sample questions for the test and you have an idea of the question format and style, try to come up with questions of your own that you can answer based on what you're reading. This will give you valuable practice applying your knowledge in the same ways you can expect to on test day.

Good luck and good studying!

Cognitive and Behavioral Perspective, Development, and Individual Differences

Jean Piaget's Cognitive Development Theory

Jean Piaget's theory of cognitive development theorizes that children will learn more effectively if they are allowed to actively adapt to the world around them through play and exploration rather than being taught skills and knowledge by others. Piaget's theory suggests that there are four major stages that children will go through as they begin to acquire new skills that will aid their ability to learn and process information independently. The four stages of cognitive development that Piaget identifies are:

- The sensorimotor stage, which spans from ages zero to two
- The preoperational stage, spanning from ages two to seven
- The concrete operational stage for ages seven to 11
- The formal operational stage for ages 11 and up

Piaget's theory is important to the study of child development because it was the first theory that recognized that children can actively and effectively learn on their own rather than being dependent on another person for learning to occur.

Review Video: Piaget's Cognitive Development Theory
Visit mometrix.com/academy and enter code: 100376

Piaget's Theory First Stage

The first stage of Piaget's theory of cognitive development, the sensorimotor stage, lasts from birth to age two.

- This is the period during which a child uses his or her senses of sight, hearing, and touch to learn about and explore elements of the world
- Using these senses, children are able to discover new ways of solving simple problems such as using their hands to drop a block into a bucket and then remove it from the bucket
- Another example is learning to use their eyes to find an object or person that has been hidden
- As a result, it is also at this stage that a child begins to develop hand-eye coordination and the ability to reason out a method of achieving goals

Piaget's Theory Second Stage

The second stage of Piaget's theory of cognitive development is the preoperational stage.

- It spans from ages two to seven
- This is the stage in which children begin to use words, symbols, and pictures to describe what they have discovered about particular elements of the world around them
- During this stage, children begin to develop an understanding of language, and they can focus their attention on a particular subject or object
- Piaget theorized that children at this stage have a faulty sense of logic when attempting to understand certain concepts such as volume, mass, and number when some element is changed

- For example, if a liquid is poured into a tall container, and then an equal amount of liquid is poured into a smaller but wider container, the children would believe that the taller container contains more liquid even though this obviously is not the case

THIRD STAGE OF PIAGET'S THEORY

The third stage of Piaget's theory of cognitive development is the concrete operational stage occurring between ages seven and 11.

- It is the stage in which a child's thinking becomes more logical regarding concrete concepts.
- In this stage, children are capable of understanding concepts of mass, volume, and number. For example, they can understand that two containers of different shapes that each have the same amount of liquid poured into them still contain the same amount of liquid despite their differences in appearance
- The child also begins to identify and organize objects according to shape, size, and color
- The child will not be able to understand more abstract concepts such as those found in calculus or algebra, however, until he or she reaches the formal operational stage of development

FOURTH STAGE OF PIAGET'S THEORY

The fourth and final stage of Piaget's theory of cognitive development, the formal operational stage, starts at age 11 and continues until the end of an individual's life.

- During this stage, an individual understands more abstract concepts and develops a logical way of thinking about those concepts. In other words, an individual begins to understand ideas that are less concrete or absolute and that cannot necessarily be backed up by physical evidence or observation such as morality, advanced mathematics, and a person's state of being
- It is also within this stage of development that individuals can understand all the variables in a problem and are able to determine most, if not all, the possible solutions to a problem rather than just the most obvious solutions
- This stage is never truly completed; it continues throughout a person's life as the individual develops and improves his or her ability to think abstractly

PIAGET'S THEORY CHALLENGED

Later researchers have challenged Piaget's theory of cognitive development because studies indicate that Piaget may have underestimated the abilities of younger children to learn and understand various concepts.

- Piaget's theory indicates that younger children are unable to understand certain concrete and abstract thoughts early within their development even if another individual teaches the child. However, this notion has been disproved.
- Research shows that young children can be taught how to handle and understand problems that Piaget believed only older children would be able to comprehend
- Researchers have also challenged Piaget's theory because studies indicate that if a younger child is given a task like one an older child might receive, but the difficulty of the task is adjusted to compensate for age, the younger child would actually understand the concept more effectively
- Piaget's theory is still important, though, because it presents the importance of active learning in a child's development
- Notably, Piaget's theory ignores many of the benefits of adult learning

Abraham Maslow's Theory

Abraham Maslow theorized that there are five types of human needs that, if arranged in order of importance, form a pyramid.

- Maslow maintained that individuals would not be able to focus on the upper layers of the hierarchy until they were first able to meet the needs at the lower layers
- The first layer of the pyramid represents the physiological needs, which are the basic needs required for an individual's survival such as food, water, breathable air, and sleep
- The second layer of the pyramid represents the safety needs, which are the elements that an individual needs to feel a sense of security such as having a job, good health, and a safe place to live
- The third layer of the pyramid corresponds to the love and belonging needs, which are needed to form social relationships such as those with friends, family, and intimate loved ones

Layers Added to Maslow Hierarchy

Maslow later added two additional layers above the self-actualization layer of the pyramid. These are the cognitive layer and the aesthetic layer.

- The cognitive layer is the layer that represents an individual's need to acquire and ultimately understand both abstract and concrete knowledge
- The aesthetic layer, which became the final layer in later versions of the pyramid, is the layer that represents the individual's need to discover, create, and experience beauty and art

Maslow later theorized that if an individual was unable to meet the needs of any given layer of the pyramid, those needs could become neurotic needs. Such needs are compulsions that, if satisfied, would not facilitate the individual's health or growth

Fourth and Fifth Layers of Abraham Maslow's Hierarchy

The fourth layer of Maslow's hierarchy of human needs is the esteem layer, which represents the individual's need to respect him or herself and be respected and accepted by others.

- The fifth and top layer of the pyramid is the self-actualization layer
- It represents the individual's need for morality, creativity, and trust
- Maslow theorized that individuals could survive without reaching the higher levels of the pyramid but that would feel a sense of anxiousness if these needs were not met
- Maslow also believed that individuals who reached the higher levels of the pyramid did not receive any tangible benefit from meeting these needs other than a feeling of fulfillment and the motivation to fulfill needs higher on the pyramid

Erikson's Psychosocial Development Theory

Erik Erikson's theory of psychosocial development breaks the process of human development into eight stages necessary for healthy functioning

- The eight stages Erikson identified are infancy, younger years, early childhood, middle childhood, adolescence, early adulthood, middle adulthood, and later adulthood
- During each of these stages, individuals must overcome a developmental obstacle, which Erikson called a crisis, to be able to progress and face the crises of later stages

- If an individual is not able to overcome one of the crises along the way, later crises will be more difficult for him or her to overcome
- Erikson's theory also maintains that individuals who are unable to successfully pass through a particular crisis will likely encounter that same crisis again

First Stage of Erikson's Theory

The first stage of Erikson's theory of psychosocial development is infancy, which spans from birth to 12 months.

- In this stage, a child is presented with the crisis of trust versus mistrust
- Although everyone struggles with this crisis throughout their lives, a child needs to be able to realize the concept of trust and the elements of certainty
- For example, a child learns that if his or her parents leave the room, they aren't going to abandon the child forever
- If a child is unable to realize the concept of trust because of traumatic life events, such as abandonment, the child may become withdrawn and avoid interaction with the rest of society

Second Stage of Erikson's Theory

The second stage of Erikson's theory of psychosocial development is the younger year's stage, which covers ages one to three.

- In this stage, a child is faced with the crisis of autonomy versus shame and doubt
- The child is presented with the need to become independent and learn skills such as using the toilet without assistance
- If the child is able to overcome this crisis, he or she will gain the sense of self-pride necessary to continue fostering the child's growing need for independence
- If, however, the child is unable to overcome this crisis and cannot establish his or her own independence, the child will develop feelings of shame and doubt about his or her ability to function without assistance

Third Stage of Erikson's Theory

The third stage of Erikson's theory of psychosocial development is the early childhood stage, spanning from ages three to five.

- In this stage, a child is faced with the crisis of initiative versus guilt
- The child is presented with the need to discover the ambition necessary to continue functioning independently
- This stage is strongly linked with the moral development of the child as he or she begins to use make-believe play to explore the kind of person he or she wants to become in the future
- If children are unable to explore their ambitions or if they are expected to function with too much self-control, they will develop feelings of guilt as they begin to see their ambitions, dreams, and goals as unattainable or inappropriate

Fourth Stage of Erikson's Theory

The fourth stage of Erikson's theory of psychosocial development is the middle childhood stage, which covers ages six to 10.

- In this stage, a child is faced with the crisis of industry versus inferiority and is presented with the need to develop the ability to complete productive tasks such as schoolwork and working in groups
- If children are unable to learn how to work effectively, either alone or in a group, they will develop a sense of inferiority as a result of their inability to complete the tasks set before them that their peers are capable of completing
- For example, if a child is regularly unable to complete their homework because the child does not understand the material while the rest of the child's peers are not having difficulty, this can lead the child to develop a sense of inferiority

Fifth Stage of Erikson's Theory

The fifth stage of Erikson's theory of psychosocial development is the adolescence stage, which covers ages 11 to 18.

- In this stage, the child is faced with the crisis of identity versus role confusion
- During this stage, the child attempts to find his or her place in society and identify future goals and the skills and values necessary to achieve those goals
- At this stage, the child also becomes more aware of how people perceive him or her and becomes concerned with those perceptions
- If the child is unable to determine what future goals he or she is interested in pursuing, it can lead to confusion about what roles the child will play when he or she reaches adulthood

Sixth Stage of Erikson's Theory

The sixth stage of Erikson's theory of psychosocial development is the early adulthood stage, which covers ages 18 to 34.

- In this stage, the young adult is concerned with the crisis of intimacy versus isolation in which an individual needs to begin establishing intimate relationships with others
- If an adult is unable to form intimate relationships with others, perhaps because of disappointing relationships in the past, this person will become more withdrawn and will isolate himself or herself from others
- Isolation can prove to be a perilous problem in the development of a healthy adult, as it prevents the individual from forming lasting relationships
- The lack of social interaction can also lead to severe personality flaws, which may hinder the development of future relationships

Seventh Stage of Erikson's Theory

The seventh stage of Erikson's theory of psychosocial development is the middle adulthood stage, occurring between the ages of 35 and 60.

- In this stage, an adult becomes aware of the crisis of generativity versus stagnation in which the individual is concerned with continuing his or her genetic line before it is too late
- Generativity refers to the ability to produce offspring and then nurture, guide, and prepare that offspring for future life
- At the same time, however, generativity in this context also refers to any act that gives something of value to the next generation such as teaching children how to read

- If an individual is unable to contribute to the next generation in some form, the individual will feel a sense of failure resulting from stagnation, which is simply a lack of accomplishment

Last Stage of Erikson's Theory

The last stage of Erikson's eight stages of psychosocial development is the later adulthood stage, which is the period that starts at age 60 and extends to the end of one's life.

- In this stage, an individual is confronted with the crisis of ego integrity versus despair
- During this time, an adult begins to examine the course of his or her life by reflecting on the kind of person that he or she has been
- If the adult feels that he or she has had a meaningful life and has accomplished something during it, this will lead to a strong sense of integrity
- However, if the individual is unhappy with the way he or she has acted, this person will experience despair and will fear death as the absolute end of further achievement

Havinghurst's Developmental Task Concept

The developmental task concept is a theory of human development established by Robert Havinghurst that states that there are certain tasks each individual needs to go through at points during his or her life to continue developing into a happy and successful adult.

- These tasks, separated into three groups by their causes, are tasks resulting from physical maturation, personal causes, and societal pressures
- A child learning to crawl is an example of a task that becomes necessary as the child matures physically
- An individual learning basic first aid because he or she is interested in becoming an EMT is an example of a personal cause
- An example of a task resulting from societal pressure is a child learning to behave appropriately in a store

The first three major age periods identified by Havinghurst in his developmental task concept are infancy and early childhood, middle childhood, and adolescence.

- Infancy and early childhood is the period from ages zero to five, and it consists of tasks such as learning to walk, talk, and eat solid foods as well as learning right from wrong
- Middle childhood is the period of development from age's six to 12 that includes tasks such as learning to get along with others, moral values, and skills and knowledge required for day-to-day living
- Adolescence is the period from ages 13 to 18, and it requires tasks that include learning how to relate with members of the opposite sex, learning the social role of one's gender in society, and preparing for life after childhood

The last three major age periods identified by Havinghurst in his developmental task concept are early adulthood, middle adulthood, and later maturity.

- Early adulthood is the period of life from ages 19 to 29, and it is the age range where tasks such as starting a long-term relationship, finding a career, and starting a family are required
- Middle adulthood is the period from ages 30 to 60 that includes tasks such as finding adult recreational activities, achieving in one's chosen career, and helping one's teenage children become healthy and happy adults

- Later maturity is the period from ages 61 to the end of a person's life
- This period consists of tasks such as adjusting to the death of a spouse, adjusting to the effects of old age, and finding people in one's peer group to interact with

Listing of Behaviors

Listing of behaviors is a techniques used to obtain an accurate count of the actual prevalence of a behavior. In using this technique in the consultation relationship, the consultant may ask the consultee to list the maladaptive behaviors of their client as well as count each time that behavior occurs. This activity serves two main purposes. First it allows the consultee to obtain a baseline measurement for the behavior. Second, it allows the consultee to see the actual number of times a behavior occurs, thus possibly changing the perception of the client's behavior. For example, the consultee may feel frustrated and state that a client always acts a certain way. After conducting the listing of behaviors activity, he may see that the client only expresses the behavior once or twice. In seeing this, the consultee will change his or her perception as well as the approach to the client and treatment.

Isolation Techniques

Isolation techniques are similar to logical consequences because these techniques are used in society, such as the consequence of imprisonment for dangerous behavior. In the classroom, isolation techniques may follow various steps or levels. At the first instance of the inappropriate behavior, the student may be required to sit silently at his seat. This step is particularly effective during group activities when other students are not in their assigned seats. During this step, the student is often given the option to participate from his seat. If the behavior continues, the next step is to increase the isolation, such as placing the student in the corner of the room to sit quietly and not participate. Following this step, the child may be asked to sit outside of the classroom if the behavior continues. In implementing the isolation technique, it is important to set specific time limits for the isolation and to follow ethical rules, such as not placing the student in a closed room.

James-Lang's Theory of Emotion

According to the James-Lang theory of emotion, our emotions are the result of our actions. This is based on the biological process of the automatic nervous system sending signals to the brain in order for the brain to process and react to a stimulus. The brain's decision to fight or flight in the case of a threatening stimulus will then trigger an emotional response, for example fear or aggression. Based on this theory, the body must undergo a physical change (i.e., increased heart rate) in order to have an emotion (i.e., fear). While this theory lends support to those emotions that are tied to physical changes in the body, it does not explain any emotional response that may result in the absence of a physical change.

Hypothalamic Stimulation

The hypothalamus has a connection to the automatic nervous system in which, when stimulated increases aggression. Work by Philip Bard, indicated this increase in aggression in studies where he stimulated the hypothalamus of a cat who responded in an aggressive attack. In addition to this finding, Bard's work revealed that some aggressive reactions were species-specific. The conclusions drawn from this work are that the automatic nervous system sends information to the hypothalamus in addition to other parts of the body during an emotional response in order to produce the appropriate physical and emotional response for a particular situation.

Conjoint Family Therapy

The first key principle of the conjoint family therapy method is to increase each family member's self-esteem with understanding of themselves and the family as a whole. Under this principle, it is important that the therapist provides the family with strategies for making changes. The second principle is to help each family member develop methods to respond calmly and effectively to conflict both inside and outside of the family structure. Finally, the therapist utilizes an experimental approach in understanding and helping the family members deal with their response and behavior patterns.

Cannon-Bard Theory of Emotion

Cannon studied the emotional responses of rats after removing various sections of their sympathetic nervous system. In doing this, Cannon was able to observe the presence of various emotions without the initial physical change experienced in the body (i.e., increased heart rate = fear emotion). Therefore, the Cannon-Bard theory of emotion includes being able to express an emotion with no physiological response initiating that emotion. Adding to this theory was the beginning of investigating the function of the hypothalamus; Cannon and Bard found that by removing this brain structure, one could stop or remove various emotional responses.

Schachter-Singer Theory of Emotion

The Schachter-Singer theory of emotion is based on cognitive feedback, which in turn determines an individual's emotional reaction. As such, the individual processes his or her surroundings and judges his or her own cognitive feedback accordingly. In other words, he uses perception of events to explain or justify reactions or feelings. Therefore, it is important to understand the notion of awareness of a physiological reaction in order to process and react correspondingly. This theory was substantiated by human studies on emotion. In such investigations, participants were told they were being studied for the effects of a vitamin on their vision. Participants were divided into groups and were injected with epinephrine or a placebo. Some were either told of the potential effects of agitation or excitability from the "vitamin shot", some were told a fabrication of possible effects, and others were not told of the effects at all. Participants were then placed in a room with an individual who behaved either excitedly or rudely. Those participants who did not know the effects of the shot or who had been deliberately misinformed, claimed to feel happy or agitated because of the other individual, not because of the epinephrine. Conversely, those who knew of the potential effects of the injection cited the drug as the source of the feeling, not the individual.

Gardner's Multiple Intelligences Theory

1. Intrapersonal intelligence is an individual's ability to process and understand his or her own emotions. Human emotions are often very complex in nature and the more intrapersonal intelligence a person has, the better he can understand and control these emotions.
2. Interpersonal intelligence refers to an individual's ability to understand the emotions of others, which is an important skill for social development.
3. Spatial intelligence is the individual's ability to understand, perceive, and manipulate the world around him through a visual-spatial context.
4. Bodily-kinesthetic intelligence is the individual's understanding of his own bodily movements as well as the ability to effectively manipulate these movements.
5. Musical intelligence is an individual's knowledge of musical functions such as pitch and rhythm.
6. Linguistic intelligence is an individual's knowledge of language, sounds, rhythm, and inflection of various words.

Microsystem, Exosystem, and Macrosystem

Microsystem

This level directly effects the development of a child and includes the child's immediate environment. This may include the nuclear and extended family, school, doctors, social services, and church.

Exosystem

This level of support does not directly affect the child's development but rather serves as an indirect support system. This may include the community's legal system, indirect social services, or friends of the family.

Macrosystem

This level of the ecological systems theory involves the values and morals of the community or society as a whole. As with the exosystem, this level does not directly influence development, but serves as an indirect support.

Classical and Operant Conditioning

Classical conditioning is a process of learning associated with behaviorism. With classical conditioning, an individual learns through the presentation of a stimulus. As such, an item is presented, followed by a stimulus, which then causes a reaction from the individual. Eventually, the individual will associate the presented item with the stimulus, even if the stimulus is no longer present. For example, object: rat, stimulus: shock to the skin, response: fear.

Operant conditioning uses rewards or punishments in order to teach a behavior. For example, a child who displays tantrums may be rewarded for every day he does not have a tantrum. The child learns that when he behaves, he receives the reward and when he does not behave, he does not receive the reward. Thus, the behavior that does not receive the reward will eventually cease.

Nature-vs. Nurture

The notion that nature is responsible for development and human behavior relies on the notion that all characteristics are inborn, they cannot be changed. Conversely, the notion that nurture is responsible for human behaviors relies on the fact that humans are influenced by learning and their environment in developing characteristics and behaviors. Therefore, characteristics and behaviors can be changed if elements of the environment are changed. While there is no solid answer as to what holds a greater influence, research on twins points to both nature and nurture playing a role in the development of behavior.

Multidimensional and Multidirectional Development

Development is considered multidimensional because all individuals grow and develop on a number of dimensions at the same time--physically, socially, emotionally, and intellectually. Likewise, development is multidirectional as development increases and declines at various points. For example, a child may be interested in sports and hone his athletic abilities, however, as he grows, his interests change to academics. Therefore, his athletic abilities may decline as his academic abilities increase. Development may also be multidirectional within the same developmental domain. For example, cognitive functioning, in general, may decline over time, but if an individual studies a specific subject, his abilities in that subject may increase.

SCHEMAS, OBJECT PERMANENCE, AND MENTAL REPRESENTATIONS

Schema is the way an individual views and thinks about the world. For example, an infant may kick his legs and make a rattle sound and become interested in the sound. As the infant grows older, he will learn that he caused the rattle by kicking and will begin to kick the rattle intentionally.

Object permanence is the cognitive ability to know that an object exists even if the object is not in view. A small child who has not yet developed object permanence may cry when his mother leaves the room because he thinks she is permanently gone. As the child develops object permanence, the crying will stop because he will know that his mother still exists and will return.

Mental representations are visual images in the mind. These may include images of people or places that the mind develops and can remember when these things are not in sight.

EARLY LANGUAGE DEVELOPMENT

Early language development begins with simple sounds. Responding to an infant's babbling and cooing will promote the continuance of these sounds. Communicating directly with a young child and engaging the child in conversations about the world around him will also encourage the child to speak and think about appropriate words for the various things he sees. Make-believe is another strategy for language development as it forces communication and discussion. Reading to children can also be a very effective way to support early language development, as the child will become exposed to vocabulary, grammar, and other aspects of language through story telling.

FREUD'S PSYCHOSEXUAL STAGES OF DEVELOPMENT

1. The oral stage, which spans from birth to one year old. During this stage the infant engages in activities revolving around oral sensations, such as sucking. According to Freud, if these oral needs are not met, oral fixations, such as thumb sucking will develop and continue into childhood and possibly adulthood.
2. The anal stage, spanning from one to three years old. This stage centers on toilet training and the child's ability or inability to hold releasing.
3. The phallic stage, spanning from three to six years old. This stage centers on the child learning of genital stimulation. Additionally, according to Freud, it is during this stage that the Oedipus or Electra conflict may develop.
4. The latency stage, from six to eleven years old. This involves the development of the superego and social development.
5. The genital stage, during adolescence. Puberty and sexual exploration occur.

HOME

The Home Observation for measurement of the Environment (HOME) is a checklist used to collect information about a child's home environment. Information for this data collection tool is gathered through observations in the home as well as through interviews with the child's parents. The focus of this scale is to determine a young child's cognitive development from birth to three years of age. There are six main subscales designed to obtain information about the emotional responsiveness of the parent, the acceptance of the parent by the child, the organization of the child's physical environment, the availability of appropriate toys, the parent's involvement with the child, and the amount and variety of stimulation.

SOCIAL REFERENCES

Social references refers to acquiring information and knowledge by observing how others response to various situations. This is a helpful tool for small children in learning on a broad scale. For example, a small child will observe how his mother responds to strangers and will learn to respond to strangers in the same way. If the caregiver demonstrates fear is a particular situation, it is likely that the child too will demonstrate fear in that or similar situations. As a child grows, he is also able to use social referencing as a means to compare his own reactions to those of others.

Temperament Types of Children

1. The easy child. This type of child has a set routine, is often happy and can easily adapt to new situations. Approximately 40 percent of children fall into this category.
2. The difficult child. This type of child does not have a regular routine, is often upset and cries often, and does not easily adapt to new situations. Approximately 10 percent of children fall into this category.
3. The slow to warm up child. This type of child is mild mannered and not very active with slower reaction times to various environmental stimuli than other children. A slow to warm up child will often have difficulty adjusting to new situations. Approximately 15 percent of children fall into this category.

While not specifically placed in a category, approximately 35 percent of children demonstrate a blend of these three temperament types.

Secure and Avoidant Attachment

Secure attachment is a healthy attachment in which the child does not experience abnormal anxiety when his parents leave. Children who demonstrate a secure attachment type are also excited and happy when their parents return. Approximately 65 percent of children fall into this attachment category.

Children in the avoidant attachment category are as unresponsive to their parents as they are to strangers. When the parent leaves, these children do not express any anxiety and will often avoid their parents when they return. Approximately 20 percent of children fall into this attachment category.

Influencing Attachment Types

Opportunity for attachment is important in developing the initial attachments as well as teaching the child positive loving affection. Research suggests that children who do not have the opportunity to develop attachments or those who develop attachments later in childhood often demonstrate social and emotional disabilities.

Quality of caregiving is another factor related to the development of attachments. Babies who have consist attention and have their needs met in a timely manner are more likely to develop secure attachment styles then those who do not have this quality of care.

Infant characteristics, specifically those tied to temperament, will play a role in the type of attachment that is developed. For example, a slow to warm up infant will also be slow to develop strong attachments with his caregivers.

Family circumstance influence the development of attachments as difficult or strained family dynamics and situations may affect the level of attention an infant receives.

Ethological Theory of Attachment

The preattachment phase spans from birth to approximately six weeks in which the child has no specific attachment but is able to recognize the mother's voice.

The attachment in the making phase spans from six weeks through six to eight months. It is during this phase that the child will begin to act differently with strangers than with his parents or other close family members.

The phase of clear-cut attachment spans from six months to two years. During this phase, the child may begin to experience separation anxiety due to the complete development of a strong attachment with his primary caregiver.

Formation of a reciprocal relationship, which spans from two years on, includes less separation anxiety, more communication, and the child's desire to become increasingly independent.

Resistant and Disorganized-Disoriented Attachment

Resistant attachment children often cling to their parents and do not make independent attempts to explore their environments. Conversely, if the parents leave and return, children with resistant attachment types will often display negative and aggressive behaviors toward the parents. Approximately 10 percent of children fall into this attachment category.

Children who display disorganized-disoriented attachment type are often the most insecure. These children may display a variety of behaviors from clinging to their parents to becoming rigid and not wanting to be held by their parents. Approximately 5 to 10 percent of children fall into this attachment category.

Memory Strategies

Memory strategies are intentions strategies for activities that an individual uses to remember new information. These may vary from rehearsing information to organizing information in such a way to make it easier to remember. The ability to develop memory strategies begins at around preschool age when children are encouraged to learn and remember their address and phone number or play memory games. Typically, at the preschool age, rehearsal is the only apparent memory strategy. As the child develops cognitively, they will increase their ability to organize information in order to remember it, thus allowing them to remember quantitatively more as well as more complex information.

Recognition and Recall

Recognition is an individual's ability to remember and determine if information presented is the same as information previously presented. Similarly, recall is the individual's ability to remember or recall information previously presented without seeing it again. For example, a child may be presented with three pictures of fruit. In the next session, he is again presented with three pictures of fruit; however, only one of the pictures was in the initial presentation. The child demonstrates recognition if he correctly chooses the target picture. In a recall situation, the picture would not be presented the second time, rather the child would be asked "Was an apple in the first set of pictures?" If the child correctly answers, he has demonstrated recall.

Conservation and Classification

Conservation is the ability to apply logical rules to problem solving and decision making. This ability typically arises during the concrete operations stage from ages seven to eleven years. A popular experiment that demonstrates this concept is as follows: the same amount of water is placed in two glasses of unequal size. A child, who is aware that the water was equal at the beginning and understands that the water is still equal, even when placed in different sized glasses, displays conservation.

Classification is the individual's ability to place information in categories or a hierarchy, as well as to determine the relationship between classified information, such as the ability to classify different types of dogs.

Sternberg's Triarchic Theory of Intelligence

Sternberg's triarchic theory of intelligence includes the componential subtheory, which follows the theory of information process and involves developing strategies, gaining knowledge, understanding metacognition, and self-regulation. Next is the contextual subtheory that suggests a goal oriented foundation of intelligence that determines the ability to adapt to, shape, and select one's environment. Finally, the experimental subtheory, involves the individual's ability to handle new situations. With the experimental subtheory, individuals who demonstrate an automatic working memory, or well ingrained memory strategies, have more room available in their working memory for the task and are thus more successful.

Emotional Self-Regulation

Emotional self-regulation is one's ability to control or regulate emotions. Young children learn to self-regulate their emotions to a certain point. For example, one strategy may be to inhibit sensory input, such as covering their eyes if they see something scary, or covering their ears if they do not like what they are hearing. Other strategies that a young child may use include talking to themselves or changing their intentions or goals. In the development of emotional self-regulation, it is important to understand the influences of temperament in this process. As such, those children with difficult temperament styles may also experience more difficulty in regulating their emotions.

Whole Language Approach

The whole language approach, according to information processing, suggests that children should learn language as a whole. In other words, as children are learning language, they should be spoken to in full, grammatically correct sentences and should be presented with similar reading materials. This approach suggests presenting all language information to a student at the same time and is similar to the development of an individual's first language.

The basic skills approach, according to information processing, suggests that students should learn language in pieces. As such, many children learn phonics or the basic sounds of the letters and letter combinations as they learn to read. With this approach, children are not presented with more complex material until they have mastered the basics.

School-Wide Positive Behavior Supports

School-wide positive behavior supports include school wide systems, non-classroom setting systems, classroom systems, and individual student system. This program also has a supplemental information system in which schools can enter discipline data online into the school-wide information system. With the school wide system, students are presented with only a few rules and expectations. These expectations for behavior are taught using direct instruction and positive behaviors are rewarded on a regular basis. Problem behaviors and consequences are clearly defined and follow through is consistently maintained. Additionally, school administrators are active members of behavior support teams, and data is collected on patterns of behaviors. Students are also expected to adhere to rules and behavior expectations in both the nonclassroom and classroom settings. At the individual level of support, students receive reinforcement and consequences for their behaviors consistently and regularly.

Phases of Behavior

1. Antecedent

The antecedent is the motivator or cue to a behavior and is required to initiate either positive or negative behavior.

7. Behavior

   The behavior is the action by the person, which may be a verbal or physical action.

8. Consequence

   The consequence is the result of the behavior. For example, a student may act out by getting out of his seat and walking around every time the class is instructed to read silently. The antecedent is reading silently. The behavior is walking around the room. The consequence may be being sent out of the room for a time out. However, by identifying the antecedent of negative behaviors, school psychologists can develop effective interventions to reduce the unwanted behavior

SCHEDULES OF REINFORCEMENT

1. Fixed interval schedule With a fixed interval schedule, reinforcement is provided at specific times on a regular basis. For example, in the classroom, a fixed interval schedule may include earning a prize on Friday for good behavior displayed throughout the week.
2. Variable interval schedule This reinforcement schedule does not rely on specific times for reinforcement, rather reinforcement is given at different times following the behavior. For example, a teacher may provide treats at the end of the day for good behavior or reward a class for good behavior following a visit to another class.
3. Fixed ratio schedule This reinforcement schedule depends on the number of occurrences of the desired behavior before reinforcement is given. For example, reinforcement may be given only after a student demonstrates seven days of good behavior in a row.
4. Variable ratio schedule This reinforcement schedule is similar to the fixed ratio schedule; however, the number of occurrences will vary. For example, the student may be rewarded after five to ten occurrences of good behavior.

BEHAVIORAL COUNSELING GOAL

The main goal of behavioral counseling is to teach the client the strategies and problem-solving skills necessary to change his or her own behaviors. In doing this, the counselor and the client analyze the problem behaviors and determine more appropriate behaviors for various situations. As the counselor uses different strategies for changing a behavior, the client should practice these strategies and should eventually be able to apply the different techniques to future situations on his or her own. Among these techniques includes teaching the client about behavioral reinforcements, which may include extrinsic and intrinsic rewards. During the beginning stages of behavioral modification, the counselor may use mostly extrinsic reinforcements. As the counseling proceeds and the client begins to learn how to modify his or her own behaviors, intrinsic reinforcement should be encouraged.

CONTINGENCY CONTRACTS

Contingency contracts are contracts developed with the child's input and include goals and objectives for changing behaviors as well as reinforcements for achieving the goals or desired behaviors. The key to using a contingency contract is the child's input, as the goals will be more effective and the child will develop a sense of ownership concerning their own behaviors. Developing a contingency contract typically involves six steps, as listed below.

1. Identify the problem.
2. Obtain a base line of the behavior through observation and data collection.

3. Agree on a set of goals for changing the behavior.
4. Develop a plan to achieve the goals.
5. Evaluate the plan at set intervals based on observable measures.
6. Modify the plan as necessary.

Self-Management

Self-management is similar to a contingency contract; however, the emphasis is placed on the child. In other words, the child takes on more responsibility in developing the behavioral plan, evaluating its effectiveness, and changing their own behaviors. The process of implementing self-management into behavioral counseling involves eight steps. All steps are completed by the child and include determining the behaviors that need changing; recording behaviors for a set period, for example, one week; determining achievable goals for the behavior change; determining and changing settings or antecedents of behaviors in order to change the behaviors; determining what consequences must change in order to change the target behaviors; recording all behaviors during the intervention period; developing rewards; and developing a plan to meet the goals.

Shaping Technique

Shaping relies on the reinforcement of desired behaviors. When using this counseling strategy, the therapist will engage in three main actions: observing, waiting, and reinforcing desired behaviors. This behavior modification strategy must be taken in small steps and requires patience because is it slightly more difficult to catch a child engaging in good behavior compared to negative behavior. Since shaping occurs over time, using a series of steps is more effective in teaching complex behaviors. Additionally, in selecting reinforcers for positive behaviors, the age of the child and the degree of the maladaptive behaviors should be taken into consideration. Extrinsic reinforcers work well with young children and, as the child masters the desired behavior, intrinsic reinforcers can be used to maintain the desired behavior.

Behavioral Momentum

Following Newton's law of motion, behavioral momentum refers to the movement of a behavior. Counselors use this behavior modification strategy for noncompliant behaviors by requesting modifications with a high probability of follow through and success. When requests for specific behaviors are complied, verbal praise is given. This is a step by step process, beginning with simple requests with a high probability of compliance in order to gain momentum, continue the desired behaviors, and eventually engage in more complex positive behaviors. Different tasks or requests are given different probabilities, such that high probability requests are those with an 80 percent change of compliance, medium probability requests have a 50-70 percent compliance rate and low probability requests have less than a 50 percent compliance rating.

Biofeedback

Biofeedback is a mechanical process that measures physiological factors of the individual, such as heart rate, muscle tension, brain waves, body temperature, and blood pressure. Using a machine to measure these processes, individuals can learn and understand bodily changes during different activities or emotional events. When used with hyperactive children, this method effectively has relaxed them. For example, a hyperactive child may be monitored using biofeedback. During a hyperactive episode, the machine will report higher levels of heart rate and blood pressure through visual and auditory means (lights and beeps). As the child learns and applies different relaxation techniques, they can see the changes in their heart rate and blood pressure in real time. In other words, by applying various techniques, the beeps and lights will slow down and the child can see the response and effect of their efforts.

Modeling as a Therapeutic Technique

Modeling refers to teaching children correct behaviors by allowing them to see the behaviors in action. Modeling can be used with real people and situations or by having the child view appropriate behaviors on TV or film. Children learn appropriate behaviors as well as the appropriate situations in which to apply the behaviors. Negative behaviors may also be learned through modeling. Additionally, both negative and positive reinforcement are effective means of developing and maintaining a desired behavior. For example, if a child knows that his peers may make fun of him if he displays a certain behavior, he will be less likely to engage in that behavior and vice versa.

Token Economies

Token economies rely on the notion of earning points, tokens, or play money to later exchange for prizes or privileges. In schools, token economies are typically used in the classroom to support classroom or positive social rules. When children in the classroom display appropriate behaviors, they will earn a token. Likewise, when children display inappropriate behaviors, they may lose their tokens. Once the child earns enough points or tokens, they can trade them in for prizes or privileges such as extra free time. Token economies can be used individually or with the class as a whole. For example, if the class displays good behavior the point or token goes to the whole class rather than just one individual.

Behavior-Practice Groups

A behavior-practice group is a group that focuses on specific behaviors, teaches individuals how to engage in these new behaviors, and provides them the opportunity to practice the behaviors. These groups provide a safe and judgment free environment for children to practice new behaviors. In developing and administering a behavior-practice group, the counselor develops a full lesson plan aimed at teaching the new behavior that also includes adequate time for practice. Additionally, the counselor will offer children feedback and teach the children how to give feedback, both positive and negative. Behavior-practice groups are most beneficial for behaviors such as study habits, communication skills, and addressing various issues related to addictions.

Role-Play

Role-play allows the child to see a situation from various points of view as well as helps them work put various decisions for each situation. Additionally, role-play allows the counselor to observe the child's reaction in various situations and determine the appropriate strategy for modifying the maladaptive behavior or decision in to a more effective behavior. In using role-play for enhancing decision making skills, the counselor will provide the child with a situation and determine where the conflict or poor decision making occurs, coach or counsel the child in positive and effective decision making, and provide an opportunity to practice the new decision making skills.

Role Reversal

Role reversal places the child in someone else's position, which allows him to see how others view his or her reactions or behaviors. For example, if a child has anger management issues and lashes out at his mother at bedtime, the role-play would involve the child playing the mother and the counselor or another individual playing the child. This set up allows the child to see his actions from an outsider's point of view as well as helps increase communication skill between the individuals involved. While this method may be helpful, younger children, those under about seven years old, will have difficulty pretending to be someone else.

Psychopharmacology

Psychopharmacology is the study of the properties, uses, and effects of various drugs to treat mental disorders. Over the past centuries, various agents, most deriving from plants and herbs have been found to treat mental disorders including depression and hyperactivity, as well as other prominent disorders found among children. For the school psychologist, it is important to understand psychopharmacology, as students with various disorders may be treated with these medications and, based on the medication a child is prescribed, may determine the counseling strategies used. Specifically, various medications work on and effect brain chemistry in different ways, which indicates different responses to treatment. It should also be noted that these medications may affect the child's academics, so children taking these medications should be closely monitored.

Doing Something vs. Saying Something

Knowing how to say something does not necessarily mean that the individual knows how to do it. When attempting to change a child's behavior, if what is being said differs from what is being done, it can have adverse affects on the child's behavior. This discrepancy can cause confusion for the child in terms of what is expected. This can be particularly true if a parent says or does one thing that models something else. Combinations of the first two points are often a major source of maladaptive behaviors in children. For example, a child may say that he can share, but in reality he does not. Focusing on sharing his toys will increase the sharing behavior more so than simply having a child say what the behavior is.

Behavior Functions

Behavior functions refer to the purpose a behavior serves. For example, maladaptive behaviors may serve the function of drawing attention; especially, if the maladaptive behavior has received attention in the past. There are four functions of behavior as described below.

1. Tangible outcomes describe behavior that results in a touchable, physically attainable prize such as a toy.
2. Social outcomes describe how behavior can result in the attainment of attention.
3. Avoidance is typically seen when a child does not or cannot do something. For example, not completing one's homework serves as an avoidance function because the child does not understand the material or does not know what is expected of him.
4. Automatic or non-socially mediated outcomes are outcomes that do not result in tangible or social outcome.

Misbehavior

Misbehaviors are those behaviors that are inappropriate in the classroom setting and cause an intended disruption. The types of misbehavior include aggression, immorality, defiance, classroom disruptions, and goofing off. Aggression is the most serious type of misbehavior and includes physical or verbal incidences intended to harm a teacher, student, or school property. Immorality includes those behaviors that go against the morals and values of society. In a classroom, this may include cheating or lying. Defiance of authority includes an intended refusal to abide by the rules set by the teacher of the school. Class disruptions may include talking out of turn or getting up and walking while the teacher is giving a lesson. Goofing off includes less serious forms of misbehavior, such as fooling around, daydreaming, or not completing assigned tasks.

Writing Stages

The first developmental stage of writing includes imitation in which young students become familiar with the concept of writing. During this stage, young students may trace letters and numbers and begin writing small words and sentences. Students typically in first and second grade will begin learning spelling strategies, handwriting, and basic grammar rules. In the next stage, typically from fourth to seventh grade, students begin more complex writing processes that require increased critical thinking, planning, and writing multiple drafts. During this phase, students also increase their ability to edit and proofread their own work. Finally, in middle and high school, the developmental process of writing becomes automatic and writing becomes a means of communication.

SELF-REGULATED STRATEGY DEVELOPMENT

Self-regulated strategy development is a highly interactive learning style. This strategy includes developing background knowledge; discussing, modeling, memorizing, and supporting it; and independent performance. This strategy is often used in student writing and includes five instructions to students:

1. Look at a picture.
2. Allow the mind to be free.
3. Write down a mnemonic for the story.
4. Write down story ideas.
5. Write the story.

These aspects and instructional steps help the student to understand the writing prompt, brainstorm ideas for this story, and develop a logical, comprehensive story. This strategy has been shown to be particularly successful in students with disabilities and learning deficiencies as well as normal students.

GLOSSARY OF MISCELLANEOUS TERMS

ACHIEVEMENT

Achievement, considered a subset of cognitive ability, refers to the mastery of declarative knowledge, knowing what to do (language based), procedural knowledge, and knowing how to do it (behavioral based). Achievement is based on prior learning and is often assessed in the classroom through criterion based testing. Additionally, many intervention models focus on achievement for monitoring and goal assessment.

ADAPTIVE/SELF HELP

Adaptive/self-help development is the ability to care for oneself, such as getting dressed on one's own.

APTITUDE

Aptitude is a considered an individual's ability or likelihood to learn. This concept relies on future learning. Aptitude is composed of more than intellectual ability and includes an individual's motivation, mental, and physical characteristics, and prior experience. Aptitude is often assessed to determine in what program a student should be placed. For example, entrance into a gifted class may require an assessment of aptitude in addition to a review of the student's previous academic achievements.

ASSESSMENT METHODS

Assessment methods include a comprehensive view of the student's behavior, including observations, review of records, biopsychosocial assessments, use of behavioral rating scales, interviews with teachers, parents, and students, and self-report measures.

ASSESSMENT SETTING

The assessment setting refers to the setting in which the discussed behavior occurs. Therefore, while the actual assessment may be conducted at school, the setting in which certain behaviors occur may actually be in the home, the assessment setting.

ASSESSMENTS SOURCES

Since this approach is a comprehensive assessment approach, information must come from various sources including the student, his parents and other family members, and teachers and other school personnel that the student has regular contact with. While information from all sources is important, the information from students in regard to their feelings is especially important. Merrell notes one exception to this would be student self-reports of very young children.

BRIEF THERAPY

Brief therapy is a therapeutic technique conducted over only a few sessions. The focus of this method is long term maladaptive behaviors.

COGNITIVE ABILITY

Cognitive ability is the ability to process information. Typically cognitive abilities fall under one of two processing systems, auditory and visual. Cognitively abilities play an important role in learning as these vary among individuals. For example, a student may have better visual cognitive abilities and benefit from seeing material presented. This student may suffer academically if a teacher uses lecture as her primary teaching method.

COMMUNICATION/LANGUAGE DEVELOPMENT

Communication/language development is the ability to accurately obtain and understand both verbal and nonverbal communication.

COMPREHENSIVENESS

Comprehensiveness requires administrators and teachers to examine all relevant interventions that may be successful for a student's academic, social, or behavioral progress.

CONSTELLATION OF BEHAVIORS

Constellation of behaviors involves measuring numerous behaviors experienced by a student, many of which may have a common underlying root.

CRITICAL INCIDENT AND DEBRIEFING

This form of therapy is focused on clients who have recently experienced a traumatic event such as a large-scale natural or manmade disaster. The therapist assists the client in dealing with the unexpected loss of property or life that resulted from the trauma.

DECISION-MAKING UTILITY

Multiple gating screening measures are proactive means for identifying students for interventions services. Therefore, the use of these measures may provide a well-rounded view of the student's strengths and weaknesses, which result in teachers' and administrators' ability to develop an effective intervention plan.

DIRECT MEASUREMENT

Using direct measurements for a behavioral assessment strategy is an effective way to determine the real world significance of student behaviors. This type of measurement strategy contrasts psychological measures that often focus only on underlined behavioral disorders irrespective of environment of occurrence. Using direct measures to assess behavior also ensures that the information gathered is meaningful and representative of the actual classroom behavior. Direct behavioral assessments conducted as a repeated observation may include observing the child's behavior while engaged in a task and not engaged in a task, on different days and at different times during the day.

DISABILITY

Disability includes deficiencies in the functioning or physical loss of a body part or an organ, which may or may not impair a student's ability to participate in the general classroom population.

EFFICIENCY

Multiple gating screening is less efficient than using pre-existing data. However, it is a more efficient screening method than individual screening.

GRIEF WORK

This type of work began with psychologists Caplan and Lindemann who provided short-term crisis intervention to survivors of a large scale fire. The focus of grief work is similar to critical incident and debriefing in that loss is addressed.

HANDICAP

A handicap is an impairment or disability with specific regard to the environment in which the individual lives, works, or goes to school. For example, a student in a wheelchair has a handicap that requires special provisions in order to ensure the equal participation (i.e., wheelchair access to classroom desk).

IMPAIRMENT

Impairment refers to all medically inactive tissue or other body part that may affect the individual's ability to complete tasks in the same manner as a non-impaired individual.

INCLUSION

Inclusion is a method of the least restrictive environment that incorporates special education teachers into the general classroom to work in conjunction with the regular teacher in order to address the needs of students. For example, a deaf student may require a sign language interpreter. Using the inclusion method, the interpreter would sit in the general classroom and assist the student.

INDIVIDUAL DIFFERENCES

Individual differences are variations present from individual to individual. In terms of cognitive abilities, individuals typically fall within a bell shaped curve, with the majority of individuals in the middle and fewer individuals to the left and right of the curve.

INTELLIGENCE

Intelligence has various definitions, however, is often defined in psychology as an individual's ability to obtain and learn information, adapt to the environment, and understand and demonstrate ability to reason.

INTER-SUBJECT RELIABILITY

The importance of inter-subject reliability on direct measurements is that children's behaviors may vary over time and repeated measures may reveal patterns in the student's behavior, thus allowing teachers and administrators to develop an effective intervention for problem behaviors.

LEVEL OF ANALYSIS

Level of analysis requires that the assessment team examines a situation at all levels, specifically examining the effects of an intervention on the big picture was well as the effects of the intervention on the details of a student's life.

MAINSTREAMING

Mainstreaming refers to the notion of the least of restrictive environment for special needs students. With mainstreaming, student with reading impairments may leave the general classroom for a short period of time in order to receive special focused education in reading; however, the student will return to the main classroom for the remainder of the day.

MOTOR DEVELOPMENT

Motor development includes both gross and fine motor skills. Gross motor skill development includes the movement of large muscles such as the ability to walk. Fine motor skill development includes use of small muscles such as the ability to write.

SOCIAL/EMOTIONAL DEVELOPMENT

Social/emotional development is the ability to effectively interact with other individuals and develop positive relationships, such as parent/child and peer relationships.

SPLITTING

Splitting, also referred to as lumping, involves the grouping of variables that fall under a common theme.

STIMULUS AND RESPONSE PATTERNS

Stimulus and response patterns also referred to as covariations, include external factors that may affect the student's progress, for example clarity of classroom rules.

TECHNICAL ADEQUACY

Multiple gating screening measures utilizes teacher's knowledge of students to determine need for interventions. While these assessments may be subjective, training on types of maladaptive behavior is beneficial.

TREATMENT UTILITY

There is little treatment utility with multiple gating screening since this strategy is focused on identification. However, teams may use collected data for baseline development and progress monitoring.

Testing, Research Design and Analysis

Student Behavior and Decision Making

1. Is the current plan achieving intended outcomes? This question examines the school's informal behavioral curriculum and identifies issues in the problem-identification stage. By asking this question, the school psychologist is able to identify whether all behavioral needs are being met and where changes in the plan's goals may be warranted.
2. What areas need improvement? After identifying areas of improvement, this question focuses on specific areas. In asking this question, a school psychologist is able to pinpoint specific areas where behavioral support is not being met.
3. Which students need additional support? This question requires a school psychologist to determine the effectiveness of the school's behavioral plan by examining students individually. This analysis will help in revising behavioral plans based on the various groups of students within the school.

Choosing Data Collection Measures

1. Data collection measures important questions. The specific data collection measures chosen for an assessment must be able to measure and provide answers to the most important questions for the student population and school being assessed.
2. Measures must be valid and reliable. In order for a measure to be valid, it must measure what it is intended to measure. A reliable measure is one that will provide consistent results.
3. Measures must be efficient. In other words, the chosen measure must be able to measure all aspects of the student population.
4. Measures must be able to demonstrate treatment utility. Each measure must be able to provide insight into intervention programs. This is important for intervention development because psychologists will base the intervention on the results of the collected data.

Selecting a Data System

One method for selecting a data system is to use previous measures. Previous measures may include previous observations, rating scales, test scores, etc. In using previous data measures, one is more likely to obtain valid and reliable measurements; however, this method is time consuming as it requires a careful assessment of various data sources. The second method is to use current measures. This method is less time consuming than the previously mentioned method, however, validity and reliability might not be established for these measures. Selection of a data system will depend on the needs and the resources of the school. Schools must also consider the time and efforts of those responsible for collecting data, which will often be the teachers and school psychologists.

Efficient Problem Solving

1. Use the scientific method to guide decision-making. Viewing the problem solving and decision-making process using the scientific method will allow the psychologist to make observations, analyze the problem, and use the information obtained from their observations to develop interventions as well as monitor and reassess progress.

2. Use direct, functional assessments. Assessments must be able to answer the right questions in order for a psychologist to develop an effective intervention. Additionally, assessments and interventions must be in line with the student's current situation. In creating a direct assessment, the school psychologist will rely on information from the student's teachers, parents, curriculum, etc.
3. Interventions match the needs of the students. Interventions that do not focus on the specific needs of the student will be ineffective. Using the various assumptions for problem-solving and developing interventions, the school psychologist will learn about the student, his needs, status in school, and will be able to determine effective interventions to meet these needs.

PROBLEM IDENTIFICATION

The ability to identify a problem is an essential skill of a school psychologist. To identify a problem, the psychologist determines the inconsistencies between the expected behavior and the actual behavior. Skills in problem identification include the following:

1. Identify the relevant behavior based on observations or other data collected, for example, teacher reports or class grades.
2. Clearly define the maladaptive behavior and develop goals and objectives to remedy the issue.
3. Establish a baseline for the behavior using data collection methods.
4. Determine an appropriate comparison for the behaviors in question in order to measure their intensity.
5. Assess the intensity of behavior to determine required level of intervention, if intervention is necessary.

FIELD BASED PROBLEM SOLVING

The problem solving method applies the scientific method to the real world environment. School psychologists can use this method to address problems, implement strategies, and assess success. There are four steps or questions that are addressed when using this method. The first step is problem identification and is necessary to determine the exact maladaptive behavior(s). Problem identification is accomplished through interviews and observations. Next, determine the cause of the behavior. In assessing the cause of a behavior, a school psychologist gains valuable information that will assist in the intervention process. The next step is the beginning stages of the intervention. A school psychologist may ask what can be done to stop the negative behavior. Finally, the intervention treatment is assessed in order to determine its effectiveness. This is a cyclic process and can be repeated until the appropriate intervention is found or when the behavior ceases.

PROBLEM-SOLVING FRAMEWORK

In the problem-solving framework, there are four levels of intervention that increase with the level of intensity of a behavioral problem. Level 1, consultation between parents and teachers, is typically informal and serves to initially address any behavioral issues a child may be demonstrating. For minor behavioral problems, this level of intervention may be effective. Level 2 in the problem-solving framework is consultation with other resources. At this level, the student is typically referred to a team of teachers, and intervention may be either informal or formal. Level 3, or consultation with an extended problem solving team, is formal and includes support from teachers and psychologists. Level 3 interventions require a specific intervention plan, follow up, and assessments. The final level of intervention is the development of an Individualized Education Plan (IEP). IEPs are developed with the participation of teachers, psychologists, parents, and the student, and serve to set specific goals and strategies for intervention. IEPs will also be assessed and revised at regular intervals.

Addressing Behavioral Problems Framework

The systems framework for addressing behavioral problems addresses groups of students, rather than individual students. This framework is the result of the No Child Left Behind Act as well as minimal funding of many school districts. At the lowest level, teachers are required to identify groups of students experiencing similar issues and address them on a universal level. When intervention begins at this level, it is proactive and, thus, considered preventative. The next level in the hierarchy of the systems framework is targeted group interventions. At this level, at-risk students are identified and referred to highly effective and quick behavioral or academic interventions. The final level of this system is individual intervention. For special cases, preventative and targeted group interventions may not be effective and the student may require one-on-one intervention. At this level, the intervention includes assessment, development of goals and objectives, intense intervention, and follow-up.

Funneling process

In using the funneling process for target variable selection, the problem is defined on a large scale and, through identification and problem solving, funneled down in order to determine the target variable. In proceeding through this process, teams work together to identify how the problem affects those involved (e.g., students). Additionally, these teams work to determine what variables can be changed in order to correct the underlying problem. Finally, the data collection process serves to assist with additional problem-solving tasks. This cyclic process continues until the academic or behavioral problem of the student or group of students is properly defined and strategies for improvement are implemented to yield specific outcomes.

Model

A model offers a general form or ideal that can be used to consider phenomena in the shared world. One organizational behavior model that can be applied to a variety of organizational types considers three levels of focus in which the organization's systems level is dependent upon the behaviors of the organization's group, which in turn depends upon individual behaviors within the groups. In this model, the individual is the foundation, and organizational systems are the highest level. Dependent and independent variables must be taken into account at all three levels. Variables that are dependent or affected by other aspects must be identified, understood or predicted. Independent variables are those that are self- regulating (that is, outside the influence of the organization) and that suggest themselves as probable causes of alterations or adjustments in independent variables. Both dependent and independent variables are found at the individual, group and systems levels.

Measuring Target Variables

The first step in measuring target variables is to develop a baseline measurement. This measurement occurs prior to the implementation of the intervention and serves to determine whether progress was made as a result of the intervention. In addition to baseline measurements, team members determine an adequate timeframe to implement the plan and measure outcomes, also called decisions rules. This process serves to provide the team with feedback on the effectiveness of an intervention plan so the team can make informed decisions concerning necessary changes to the plan. Finally, the level of intervention and monitoring depends on the level of the problem. For example, when providing intervention for high-risk behavioral problems, monitoring will occur daily, while low-risk problems may be monitored weekly or biweekly.

Selecting Target Variables

1. Variables are clearly defined using operational definitions. This means that the variable can be observed and measured.
2. Variables can be changed significantly through the selected intervention, for example, GPA.
3. Variables can be measured directly, meaning that the selected target variable has a direct connection to the problem behavior.
4. Variables are reliable, or measure what they intend to measure.
5. Variables link present and future outcomes in a meaningful way. In other words, the variable is valid and will measure the same construct each time.
6. Variables are examined though functional hypotheses. This is typically accomplished by connecting information about the problem with possible variables to develop an intervention.
7. Variables are prioritized and combined. Different variables may affect the student in different ways. Additionally, variables may affect the same behavior. In prioritizing and combining variables, teams can more effectively and efficiently narrow problem variables.

Selecting Students for Referral

One of the most common problems in selecting students for referral and intervention has been the inconsistency in guidelines for selection. Traditionally, educators wait until a student demonstrates problems or falls behind academically before any action is taken. This practice has resulted in an ineffective referral process and an overrepresentation of certain minority groups receiving intervention. Adding to the issue of student selection is the use of self-referral. While this strategy does have its advantages, it is very subjective and enhances the variance in the referral and intervention process. Developing clearly defined referral processes is important, however, referral may continue to contain some level of bias, especially in terms of behavioral problems.

Selecting Students for Intervention Services

1. Teacher nominations are very useful in the selection process because these individuals have firsthand knowledge of the students' strengths and weaknesses. However, due to variations in teacher expectations and tolerance for behavioral problems, these referrals may, at times, be biased.
2. National norms are a common method for student selection and are useful in comparing students with their same age and same grade peers. However, using national norms does not account for specific demographics and overall student climate of an individual school.
3. Using educational indicators is based on extensive research and therefore offers educators a valid and reliable tool for selection. In using this method of selection, educators must carefully assess the indicators for educational risk, as a student may demonstrate an indicator but not necessarily be affected by the risk factor.

Base Rate

A base rate is the frequency of risk characteristics, which may include socioeconomic, social, academic, or behavioral issues. In determining the base rate for a student, educators are able to determine the necessary intervention methods as well as appropriate variables for measurement. School wide and demographic based ratings are also a useful practice for determining the effectiveness of interventions. In cases where base ratings are high, administrators may consider implementing school wide intervention programs. This may include school wide programs for reducing violence or teen smoking. On the other hand, in schools where base ratings are low, administrators can focus on specific groups or individuals for intervention services. This may include developing IEPs for students with special learning needs.

STUDENT OUTCOME MEASURES

Student outcome measures assess student progress through the academic curriculum. These are important in early identification of academic problems. One way student outcomes are measured is through static measurements. These measurements are comparisons between where the student is academically and a set milestone of where the student should be. For example a reading milestone for a student in kindergarten may include being able to read 100 site words by a specific point in the school year. At the set point, the student would be assessed on his ability to read site words and his score would be compared to the milestone (e.g., 100 words). A second type of outcome measurement is through learning trajectories. This outcome measurement is based on a comparison of the student's current learning trajectory with that required in order to reach learning milestones. Learning trajectories may also be based on the learning trajectories for students who are not at academic risk.

RTI

Response to Intervention takes a proactive approach to intervention by providing intervention in the classroom prior to a referral as soon as a problem is noticed by the teacher. This method was developed from the No Child Left Behind Act and calls for the screening of all students. This is different from traditional intervention selection procedures where screening and intervention is not implemented until a need is identified and a referral is made. Following a school wide assessment, RTI identifies those in need of intervention services and immediately provides students with necessary interventions. Interventions with RTI are empirically based, with operationally defined and measureable variables. Regular assessments are conducted to ensure students are meeting goals and, once goals have been met, intervention may be concluded.

RTI TIERS

The first tier of RTI includes the school wide basic instruction and behavior management. Tier 1 typically addresses the academic and behavioral needs of 80-90 percent of students. When students' needs exceed what is provided at the school wide level, they are moved to Tier 2 assessment and intervention. Tier 2 begins the implementation of targeted interventions and addresses the needs of 5-10 percent of at-risk students. These interventions are assessed and revised as needed on a regular basis. If Tier 2 interventions are not adequate, a student may be referred for Tier 3 intervention. This level of intervention includes intensive, individual attention, and accounts for approximately 1-5 percent of at-risk students.

INTERVENTION PROGRAM

1. Role identification of all shareholders must be clearly defined. These roles will include the administration, teachers, school psychologists, students, and parents involved.
2. Accurate problem identification includes ensuring the intervention addresses the identified problem as well as the overall goals of the school in terms of student success.
3. Integrity of the implementation plan refers to the viability of the plan being implemented. The proposed intervention plan must be applicable and achievable both in terms of the teachers' and the student's expectations and abilities.
4. Effective identification of measureable variables will ensure that progress monitoring is efficient and accurately monitors the goals put in place by the plan.
5. Identification of a lead team member will ensure that the daily activities and issues regarding the implementation plan are followed.

Obtaining and Examining Screening Data

1. Select valid screening measure. This step ensures that the measure coincides with classroom expectations and measures the students' abilities according to their grade and age. Often times, comparisons with milestones or other academic norms will be used and are considered valid.
2. Specify comparison criteria. During this step, intervention teams will compare a student's current academic or behavioral standing with a future, desired outcome. These comparison criteria may be obtained from data from the school's previous year or from the research literature.
3. Interpret screening data. During this step, educators may look at a single measure or may need to look at an overall view of the student's academic profile. Additionally, intervention teams must determine if screening data should be examined on a school wide or individual basis.
4. Presenting screening data. This stage will provide the implementation team with a visual graph of the current academic and behavioral climate of the school or classroom. Outliers, or those students falling below established criteria, can then be easily identified.

CHC Theory

Cattell-Horn-Carroll (CHC) theory is based on a combination of empirical evidence collected from behavioral factors including developmental, neurocognitive, and genetic research. The basis of this theory is the classification of intelligence and cognitive abilities into three levels, or stratum, of a hierarchy. Stratum I includes narrow abilities, which, more specifically, is 70 specialized abilities. Some of these narrow abilities include phonic coding, memory span, and working memory. Stratum II includes broad abilities, fluid reasoning, short-term memory, and cognitive processing speed. Finally, Stratum III includes general intelligence and refers to the general amount of declarative and procedural knowledge an individual possesses or has the ability to acquire. Using the CHC theory, educators focus of obtaining a comprehensive assessment of the student's past, present, and future academic picture.

Phonological Deficits

When first assessing a student for phonological deficits, a teacher should determine the type of deficit, the magnitude of the deficit, and the appropriate instruction to address the deficit. One important assessment task is to determine the developmental process of phonological learning. This will further assist school psychologists and educators in developing an appropriate intervention plan. One common tool in reading and phonological assessment is the use of DIBELS (Dynamic Indicators of Basic Early Literacy Skills). This assessment tool is geared toward preventing students from falling behind in phonological development by serving as an early warning system. Assessment tools such as the DIBELS also can be used to monitor interventions and assess a student's progress.

NWF Measure

The Nonsense Word Fluency (NWF) measure assesses the student's ability to correctly verbalize nonsense words. For this assessment, the student is provided with a list of nonsense words and asked to verbalize each letter of the word or the word as a whole. This is a timed assessment as students have one minute to correctly identify as many nonsense words as possible. Students, who are skilled at grouping phonemes, will score high on this task, as they will be able to efficiently and accurately pronounce each word. One the other hand, students unable to use phonetics may only verbalize the letters individually and thus score lower. Scores on the NWF are often compared to criterion based or normative scores. These scores can also be used as a baseline measure prior to the implementation of an academic intervention.

Reading Fluency

Reading fluency is the ability to read accurately and quickly, and use appropriate expression. Included with reading fluency is comprehension. The three subcomponents of reading fluency include automaticity, reading rate, and prosody. Automaticity is the function of reading speed and accuracy. Associated with automaticity is reading rate, which is the student's ability to decode and read the text. Finally, prosody refers to the expression used in reading. A student with high reading fluency will be able to quickly read site words, decode more difficult words, and read with expression according to the punctuation included in the text. While these are all subcomponents of reading fluency, automaticity is the foundation of this skill. As such, students who struggle with automaticity will also struggle with prosody.

General Outcome Measures

General outcome measures refer to overall outcomes as defined the school's curriculum. These measures are often associated with mathematics instruction and have, when properly monitored, shown improvements in student achievement. Subskill mastery measures, on the other hand, refer to specific skills associated with a topic. Monitoring this subskill mastery is particularly important in mathematics because each concept builds on the previous one. In monitoring subskill mastery, teachers are able to determine specific difficulties and initiate the intervention process when difficulties arise. Subskill mastery measures are also helpful in determining what material is presented in the curriculum. For example, if an entire student population struggles with a specific topic, this may be an indication that the topic is too advanced, and teachers and administrators are able to reassess the curriculum.

Multiple Gating Screening Measures

Stage 1, also referred to as Gate 1, involves school-wide screening. It is during this screening process that individual students and groups of students in need of more intense screening and intervention are identified. The most commonly used screening method involves the teachers rank ordering students according to need. This process is also called Systematic Screening for Behavioral Disorders (SSBD).

Stage 2 involves taking the rank ordering information from Stage 1 and rating the top students according to their level of externalizing and internalizing maladaptive and adaptive behaviors.

Students will move on to Stage 3 if they are below norms based on characteristics and checklists used in Stages 1 through 3. Once identified in Stage 3, students are referred to expert observers for assessment and monitoring.

Behavioral and Emotional Rating Scale

The Behavioral and Emotional Rating Scale is used with students ages five through eighteen. The goal of this scale is to measure the strengths of the student including interpersonal, family, intrapersonal, school functioning, and affective strengths. This scale is typically completed by someone who knows the child well, and may include a teacher, parents, or school staff members. The Behavioral and Emotional Rating Scale is particularly useful for students with severe emotional and behavioral disorders. Items included in this scale load on five different factors; however, some researchers question the validity of these factors and suggest conceptual models be developed to further validate the measure. Validation is particularly important since recent versions of these measures have been developed separately for parents and teachers; however, the factors have not been validated for variations in these groups.

Walker McConnell Scale of Social Competence and School Adjustment

The Walker McConnell Scale of Social Competence and School Adjustment has been normed for use with students in grades kindergarten through sixth. This scale is useful for identifying students with social-behavioral adjustment problems, distinguishing at-risk students from not at-risk students, and developing intervention plans for identified students. Forty-three items are rated on a six-point Likert type scale with two subscales for adaptive classroom behavior and interpersonal social skills. While some research indicates that this scale has good internal and external validity, some suggests that the Walker McConnell Scale of Social Competence and School Adjustment has not been normed on a representative sample of the United States population. This factor raises issues in the scale's reliability for use among all student populations including various ethnic groups.

Positive Behavioral Referrals

Positive behavioral referrals focus on acceptable school behaviors and give recognition to students engaging in these behaviors. In giving recognition to positive behaviors, schools may offer students tickets or recognition cards displayed throughout the school. Using positive behavioral referrals also helps administrators track positive to negative behavioral referral ratios. However, little research is available to suggest the usefulness of these referrals in developing valid monitoring and intervention plans. Additionally, referrals are often subjective, thus leaving these referrals open to bias. The use of subjective measures for referrals suggest poor reliability as referrals are based on teachers' understanding of the referral process, personal biases, and classroom expectations. However, recognition for positive behaviors may give students incentive to continue these behaviors.

Prosocial and Maladaptive Behaviors

School-wide observation systems assess prosocial and maladaptive behavior including peer and student-teacher interactions. Intervention teams use the information gathered from these observations to determine the level of needed intervention concerning when and where maladaptive or prosocial behaviors occur. Specifically, intervention decisions are made by determining probabilities of when and where certain behaviors will occur. While this type of observation is often not cost effective on a school wide level, if administrators and teachers have a basis for needed observations (i.e., reoccurring school wide or individual incidents) they can focus their efforts in those areas. For example, if maladaptive behaviors tend to occur in the classroom, observations can focus in this area and teachers can look into classroom management techniques, classroom expectations, teaching methods, and classroom rules as sources of the behavior.

Social Emotional Skill

Social emotional skill inventories can be used by teachers to assess classroom social behaviors based on grade-level expectations. Using checklists and rating scales, teachers can determine students' strengths and weaknesses in terms of social responsibility and social behaviors. These inventories can also be used to determine if classroom or individual interventions are needed to address deficiencies and social skills. While these inventories are useful in the classroom, they are subjective measures that will vary by teacher, classroom, and student population; therefore, reliability and validity of social emotional skill and inventories is questionable and must be developed based on the needs of individual schools. Due to the additional paperwork involved in with these inventories, this strategy may not be time or cost effective for all schools.

Assumptions for Behavioral Assessments

1. Environmental conditions may determine behaviors expressed by students. For example, students may demonstrate maladaptive behaviors in the classroom, but these behaviors may be nonexistent at home or on the playground.
2. Behavior serves as the focus of an assessment rather than simply an indicator of a potential disorder. In placing the behavior as the focus of the assessment, teachers and administrators are able to directly address the behavioral issues present and develop intervention plans to correct these behaviors rather than trying to treat for an underlying behavioral disorder.
3. Repeatedly collecting data on the environment in which a behavior occurs is a necessary component to determining maladaptive behaviors.
4. By altering conditions, such as antecedents, behaviors may change. This is an important component in developing a behavioral intervention, as teachers and administrators can determine what antecedents will produce positive behaviors rather than maladaptive behaviors.

Situational Specificity Distinctions

It is impossible to observe and collect data on all behaviors. Therefore focusing on a subset of behaviors that have been suggested as indicators of the behavioral problem is a more efficient way in determining the behavioral problem and in developing an appropriate intervention. There are, however, differences between how this information is interpreted in terms of the psychological or behavioral assessment. For example, psychological assessments focus on an individual's personality characteristics that may be predictors of a behavior. Additionally psychological assessments gather information based on single points in time and do not look it overall situation specific behaviors. On the other hand, the behavioral assessment simply focuses on the actual behaviors in specific settings.

Inadequate Classroom Instruction

The three main factors of inadequate classroom instruction include curriculum materials that are not appropriately matched for the grade level, a teacher's inability to adapt or customize instruction materials to meet the students' level of understanding and needs, and a lack of clear and effective classroom rules and procedures. In terms of inappropriate classroom materials, research has found that materials that are too difficult or above grade level abilities often result in frustration. Likewise, materials that are below the students' abilities may lead to boredom. Teachers who fail to adjust course materials have a poor understanding of the step-like progression students go through during the learning process. These teachers and students may experience frustration during the learning process because of too high or too low expectations of learning. Finally, developing clear and consistent classroom rules allows all students to understand what is expected of them and the consequences of disobeying those rules

Internalizing Problems

Internalizing problems are those that cause significant mental distress and may include depression, anxiety, somatic problems, or social withdrawal. In addition to specific disorders such as major depression, bipolar, obsessive compulsive, or panic disorders, internalizing problems may also include specific thoughts such a suicidal or self injury. Other factors of internalizing problems are tendencies to have a comorbidity with other disorders or symptoms. There are a number of challenges for the school psychologist in terms of identifying an internalizing problem. First, the characteristics or symptoms associated with internalizing problems are often not overly observable. Second, school psychologists typically are not made aware of students with internalizing problems as these students are referred less often than the students with externalizing problems. A third challenge for the school psychologist is training on comprehensive assessments for students with internalizing problems. Finally, there is little research offering links between assessment measures and interventions for students with internalizing problems.

English Language Proficiency

English language proficiency deals with the content knowledge and skills of the English language rather than actual language knowledge and skills. More specifically, English language proficiency consists of the skills that are necessary for a student to participate fully in the academic environment. It is important to understand that the development of English language proficiency must extend past ESL teachers and benefits from the support and encouragement of all teachers with whom the student is involved. Additionally, English language learners have a variety of education histories, levels of understanding, social experiences, and cultural and economic status. While practices of English language proficiency programs will vary among states and school districts, it is important that all schools implement a comprehensive plan with established standards of learning and clearly defined populations in need, as well as the domains of language, including listening, speaking, reading, and writing.

Functional Behavioral Assessment

Functional behavioral assessments allow school psychologists to determine the pattern of antecedents and consequences revolving around certain behaviors. Additionally, functional behavioral assessments help to determine what antecedents and consequences are functionally related to the behavior during specific situations, which may be changed or manipulated resulting in a change of the child's behavior. It is important to determine both the antecedents and consequences of the behavior in order to avoid negative reinforcement of these behaviors. For example, the antecedent of the disruptive behavior is group work and the consequence of that disruptive behavior is being sent out into the hallway. A certain student does not like group work, so he acts up, and is sent into the hall. He has succeeded in getting out of the group work and a negative behavior is reinforced.

Testing-Bias, Content Bias, and Slope Bias

Testing bias refers to an assessment or testing instrument's degree to which a group's score is affected by factors not related to the constructs being tested. For example, a reading assessment may pose testing bias for students whose first language is not English. In this case, the student may have no deficiencies reading in their native language; however, when tested in English, may indicate reading deficiencies.

Content bias refers to actual content items on an assessment or testing instrument causing bias due to its irrelevance to certain cultures or subgroups. For example, low-income students may not see the relevance of a test question that discusses flying on an airplane.

Slope bias refers to mean scores predicting performance differently for different groups obtaining the same score. For example, if Group 1 and Group 2 are given the same test, scores from Group 1 may predict a grade of an A, whereas the same score from Group 2 would predict a grade of an F.

Skill and Performance Deficits

Skill deficits are deficits in the student's abilities to be academically successful. This type of deficit typically cannot be directly observed as often serves an antecedent for other maladaptive behaviors. For example, a student may act out during a class activity because he does not know how to complete the activity or does not know what is expected of him. In cases such as these, the teacher must rely on indirect observations to determine the deficit.

Performance deficits are deficits in the student's ability to perform a skill accurately and consistently. While a student may know the information, they do not always apply the information correctly. Performance deficits typically stem from a lack of motivation. For example, a student knows his math facts; however, does not like math, and may at times show poor performance. In this situation, increasing the student's motivation will help in addressing this type of deficit.

POSITIVE AND NEGATIVE REINFORCEMENT

Positive reinforcements are rewards or positive attention granted when a student performs or behaves well. In the classroom, special treats such as sitting in a special chair or extra free time may serve as positive reinforcements for students to perform and behave well.

Negative reinforcements strengthen performance and behavior, and typically involve the removal of a negative condition. Suppose a college student saw the weather forecast for rain and packed an umbrella. The next day the student didn't notice The forecast for rain again and didn't pack an umbrella. The student then spent the day walking between classes being cold and wet. The behavior of checking the weather forecast is strengthened by the consequence of being unprotected in the elements.

SCREENING TO ENHANCE EQUITABLE PLACEMENT MODEL

The Screening to Enhance Equitable Placement model was designed using the problem solving approach to develop intervention strategies and assess interventions in order to determine success of the interventions and additional needs for CLD students. Under this program, CLD students may be identified as at-risk and referred to school-based intervention teams for assessment. Using the problem solving approach, school-based teams will assess the student, determine necessary intervention approaches, implement interventions, and conduct regular programming evaluations to determine the effectiveness of the intervention implemented. While the STEEP the model has been thoroughly used and validated within the African American population, this model has not been validated among English language learners.

AUDIOLINGUAL APPROACH

This method of English language learning developed in the United States during World War II. The underlying theory behind the audiolingual approach is that one must rehearse the language on a regular basis as well as receive reinforcement. This method consists of three main components. Practice, the first component, involves memorization using situation-based prompts. Drills provide the reinforcement for the practice. Finally, learning must be reinforced with conversations in the study language. Since the inception of this method, which was originally oral, written materials have been introduced as supplemental learning material.

RATIONAL FOR SCHOOL-BASED ASSESSMENTS

With the increased interest in students with disabilities and the passing for various educational legislation aimed at ensuring that these students receive equal education, school-based assessments are useful in determining if a school is meeting the needs of its students as well as adhering to the educational legislation. In addition to general curriculum assessments, behavioral assessments are also necessary to illuminate how the students' emotional and behavioral health affects their academic progress. These assessments also help educators to develop effective interventions and curriculum.

Design-Based Research Collective

The Design-Based Research Collective developed five guidelines that integrate theoretical research with practical application of program development and assessment. It is necessary to combine the goals to improve the program with those used in developing theories about the program's functions. Additionally, program developers must work in cycles including design, implementation, program assessment, and redesign. Based on the development and assessment of a program, usable theories will emerge, which should be shared with the community. During this process, developers must also take into consideration how the program works in practical settings. Finally, effective program developers will document their process and share their findings with the community.

Bilingual and ESL Program Participation

Since there are various ESL programs throughout the United States, it is important to determine to what extent the student has received English instruction. For example, the student in an English-only program will have been exposed to more hours of English language than a student in a transitional bilingual program.

Current Language Proficiency

This information will be gathered from teacher interviews, assessments, and reviews of the student's academic record. Language proficiency can be determined by the language that the student uses most frequently for reading, writing, and speaking. Language proficiency assessment should be conducted for all languages the student knows how to speak. Collecting current language proficiency information will help the intervention team in developing appropriate program goals and assessment methods.

Level of Acculturation

Information on level of acculturation refers to the extent to which a student is acculturated to society. A student's understanding of mainstream society is relevant and important in the classroom and can be used to determine appropriate instruction, methods of assessment, and interventions. For example, the student may have a high level of English proficiency in terms of being able to read and speak English; however, a low level of acculturation will result in the inability to appropriately use the English language in context. Considerations, in terms of level of acculturation, include the extent to which the classroom curriculum is based around cultural information relevant to the student, sensory and communicative impairments of the student, extent of formal education as well as any significant breaks from education, and the family's cultural views of education.

Eliminating Bias Against ESL Students

Bilingual personnel should be fluent in all languages the student speaks as well as be able to administer and analyze assessments in these languages. Bilingual personnel should be able to appropriately modify, translate, and administer assessments that are not otherwise representative of the student. Such modifications may be necessary in order to eliminate bias during the assessment and testing phase in order to gain an accurate understanding of the student's abilities. All English-speaking specialists should be trained by the bilingual personnel on all assessment measures necessary, including those measures that may need to be translated or modified. Finally, it may be necessary to use an interpreter for those administering nonverbal or performance intelligence assessment measures in any language other than English or Spanish.

Providing Effective Multicultural Consultation

1. Understanding one's own and others' culture. In understanding one's own culture, the individual is able to gain a sense of identity and self-awareness of possible prejudices and assumptions of others. Understanding other cultures allows the individual to empathize with other perspectives and values.
2. Developing cross-cultural communication and interpersonal skills. This factor allows an individual the ability to accurately communicate education information and program advantages and disadvantages across cultures.
3. Examining the cultural embeddedness of consultation. This is the consultant's ability to view and discuss information from the student or client perspective.
4. Using qualitative methodologies. This is the consultant's ability to effectively collect, assess, and interpret data concerning programs that will be a benefit to the bilingual education program of their schools

American Sign Language, Manually Coded English, and Finger Spelling

American Sign Language is a commonly used language among deaf individuals in America. This language uses a variation of hand gestures and movements, facial expressions, and body postures in order to communicate. For deaf students, the use of American Sign Language during identification and assessment procedures may be a useful tool for accurately assessing the student's language abilities. American Sign Language also has its own grammatical patterns, which must be taken into consideration during the assessment process.

Manually coded English is a form of sign language that follows the same grammatical rules as spoken English and therefore individuals can sign and speak at the same time.

Finger spelling uses finger and hand positions to create the 26 letters of the alphabet. Individuals may also trace letters in the air or on the hand in order to spell out the words they wish to speak.

Medical Model of Disability

Medical model of disability includes the view of an individual's disability not defined in the social context but rather in the physical or mental context.

Regular education classroom refers to the classroom attended full-time by all students who are not designated with a disability and attended part time by students designated with disabilities (when those students are not learning in the special education classroom).

Service delivery model refers to the intervention or special education services provided to a child in order to meet the child's special needs. These services may be provided in the regular education classroom or outside the regular education classroom for specified periods during the school day.

Social construction model of disability defines students with disabilities in terms of social factors such as interpersonal relationships.

Research Process

1. Identifying the research problem includes determining issues or situations that need to be addressed by educators in order to improve the education system.
2. Review of literature includes a thorough review of past studies that are related to the research problem being addressed.
3. Identifying the purpose for the research states the researcher's intent of an investigation and proposes the hypothesis.

4. Data collection includes conducting the study, making observations, and collecting qualitative or quantitative data.
5. Analyzing and interpreting data. During this step in the research phase all collected data is statistically analyzed in order to determine significant information regarding the research question.
6. Reporting and evaluating research. All above steps are presented to the other researchers, educators, and policy makers. In evaluating the research, additional studies may be conducted to verify information gathered in the original study.

Research Ethical Practices

1. Respecting the rights of participants. This ethical practice can be found in the ethical standards of the American Educational Research Association as well as the American Psychological Association's ethical guidelines. In respecting the rights of participants, researchers must understand and disclose any negative effects a study may have on an individual as well as honor the participants' confidentiality with all information collected during the study.
2. Honoring research sites. Research may be conducted in a number of places. Researchers conducting a study in a place such as a school should be granted permission prior to beginning their study and should create as little a disturbance as possible.
3. Reporting research fully and honestly. Regardless of results, the researchers should provide a full and honest report of all data collection and analyses. By providing an honest report, the researcher increases understanding of what is actually going on concerning the research problem.

Quantitative and Qualitative Research

Quantitative research involves asking specific questions and collecting numeric data in order to address these questions. Following data collection, researchers will analyze all information using statistics in order to obtain an unbiased and objective view of the research question. Also referred to as empirical research, quantitative research typically involves making comparisons and drawing cause and effects from the results.

Qualitative research involves gathering subjective information through interviews and general questions. This information typically is not analyzed using statistics and is often subjective and biased. This research method depends on exploratory analysis and understanding in terms of identifying the research problem and utilizing the literature. Data collection is likely based on participant experience, collecting general, written, or verbal information from only a few participants, and identifying themes in the data. Qualitative research is often subjective and biased.

Experimental Research Design

Experimental research design is a quantitative research method that relies on the use of collecting data using interventions or group comparisons to address the research question. In an experimental design, the researcher will identify two or more groups, one being a control group that receives no intervention and the other being an experimental group that does receive an intervention. For example, to address the effectiveness of a reading intervention, the researcher may divide a class into two groups, one who receives the reading intervention and the other who does not receive the intervention. After a set period of time, information will be gathered from both groups and compared and analyzed to determine group achievement is different. Experimental design can also be used with one group using the pre and posttest method. This involves collecting a baseline measure of the group, providing an intervention, and collecting a post intervention measure to determine effectiveness. Experimental designs are useful in revealing cause and effect; however, they can be costly, require a large number of participants, and are time consuming.

Correlational Research Design

Correlational research design is a type of quantitative research method that compares associations and relationships of variables. The purpose of determining correlations is to build a basis for predicting outcomes. In other words, when two or more variables are correlated, researchers can determine future outcomes of one variable based on information of the other. For example, correlational research has helped determine that SES may negatively affect academic success. Therefore, rather than assessing all students, a school may indentify potential at-risk students based on the SES variable. This type of research design is effective in schools as it requires only a single group and may be more cost effective and less time consuming than other research methods. However, results from correlational research must be interpreted with care as confounding variables may affect findings.

Explanatory and Prediction Design

Explanatory research design focuses on examining how changing one variable affects changes on another variable. This research design involves collecting data from a single point in time; information about past or future variables are not a concern. The researchers also collect data only from a single group, collecting at least two scores or pieces of information from each individual of the group; one score for each variable.

Prediction design aims to predict the outcome based on certain variables, also called predictors. With this research design, the researchers will use predictor variables and criterion variables. Criterion variable refers to the desired outcome of the research. For example if a researcher wants to determine the success of student, he will determine predictor variables such as the previous year's grade point average and the criterion variable, such as required grade point average, that define successful completion.

Grounded Theory Research Design

Grounded theory research design is a qualitative research method that uses a systematic design to explain a process or action of a specific issue. Grounded theory design and the use of systematic data collection procedures allow researchers to identify categories, draw connections between the categories, and form theories that explain the processes examined. Results from this theory are said to be grounded in data and have practical applications in various settings. The use of grounded theory research design can help researchers determine developmental processes of students or interactions among individuals. Additionally, due to its step-by-step nature, results from data analysis in one step can help determine the appropriate data analysis for the next step.

Systematic Design Approach

The systematic design approach relies on the use of steps within the data analysis phase, which include open coding, axle coding, and selective coding. In the first phase, open coding, researchers develop categories based on the data collected, for example, interviews and observations. All data collected is divided into a select a category. Within each category are subcategories, also called properties that provide specific details for each category. During the second phase, axle coding, the researcher selects a category from the open coding phase and defines it as the core phenomenon in order to draw relationships between this category and the remaining categories. Visual aids depict this phenomenon and result in a diagram called a coding paradigm. In the final phase, selective coding, the researcher will develop a theory based on the relationships of the categories from the axle coding phase.

EMERGING DESIGN AND CONSTRUCTIVIST DESIGN

Emerging design is based on the idea that the theory should emerge organically from the data collected, rather than the researcher choosing categories in which to place the data. With this design method, the researcher will not develop a coding paradigm and the information will be more flexible for developing a theory. The basis for the emerging design is that data collected from grounded theory research design is abstract, information is not forced into a category, and this data may represent a more practical view of the situation.

Constructivist design relies on the researcher's explanations of the data collected rather than simply predetermined categories. In order for the researcher to provide such explanations, responses are collected from various questions which are specific to the data. Of note, results using this method are merely suggestions and are often inconclusive.

MIXED METHODS RESEARCH DESIGN

A mixed methods research design approach uses both qualitative and quantitative research paradigms. Disadvantages to using this approach include a lack of understanding of both of these research methods, the process is time consuming, and requires extensive data collection. However, using both quantitative and qualitative information will help the researcher gain a comprehensive picture of the research problem. With mixed methods research, the researcher can use qualitative information gained through interviews or observations to provide additional support for the quantitative information gathered from numerical data collection. Additionally, some researchers may use this type of research design as a multiphase study. For example, a researcher may gather qualitative information to begin building a basis for the research question and then collect quantitative data to support their questions or hypotheses.

TYPES OF MIXED METHODS RESEARCH

1. Triangulation design - This process requires collecting quantitative and qualitative data simultaneously, and combining the results to gain a comprehensive understanding of the problem. The key characteristic of this design approach is that equal priority is given to both types of data and results are compared and contrasted between both types of data.
2. Explanatory design - This design method uses a two phase model in which priority is given to quantitative data collection. The second phase includes a limited qualitative data collection piece. Following all data collection, the results from the qualitative phase serve to support and refine information gathered from the quantitative phase.
3. Exploratory design - This is a multiphase research method that places an emphasis on the qualitative data during the first phase. Quantitative data is collected during the second phase and is used to support and explain findings from qualitative phase.

SURVEY RESEARCH DESIGN

Survey research design is a quantitative research method that involves administering surveys in order to determine individuals' attitudes or opinions about a topic. Surveys may be delivered face-to-face, pen and paper, over the phone, and most recently, over the Internet. With this method, no mental treatment or intervention is administered; therefore, researchers cannot determine cause and effects of any specific variables. The specific purpose of survey research design is to identify trends in the data rather than to offer specific explanations for behaviors, attitudes, or outcomes. Surveys often provide researchers with general information about a population and may be helpful as a first step in determining research questions for additional experimental research.

TYPES OF SURVEY DESIGNS

1. Cross-sectional survey designs are point-in-time surveys collected from a representative sample of the population. A cross-sectional design may aim to examine current attitudes, beliefs, opinions, or practices; compare two or more groups; measure community needs; or evaluate the program.
2. Longitudinal survey design involves collecting information within the same population over a period of time. For example, if researchers wish to determine the satisfaction of a newly implemented program over a period of five years, they may survey students involved in the program at the beginning, in the middle, and at the end. Results will then be compared among the three time points. Within longitudinal survey design are trend studies and panel studies.

ETHNOGRAPHIC RESEARCH DESIGN

Ethnographic research design uses the qualitative research approach to interpret a cultural group's pattern of behaviors, beliefs, and language as they have developed and changed over time. Culture is the basis of this research design method, which can be defined as including language, rituals, economic structures, communication styles, and lifestyles of a particular group. In using this research method, the researcher can define culture in a broad way. For example, researchers who may wish to examine the culture of a school would include the entire school, students, teachers, staff, administrators, etc; or for a more narrow examination, teachers only. Like other qualitative research paradigms, ethnographic designs rely on subjective information from individuals. While this research method can provide an overview of what a culture comprises, results cannot be used to predict outcomes or determine cause and effect relationships.

Types of ethnographic research designs

1. Realistic ethnographies are narrative and in the third person, providing an objective view of a situation. This information is based on the researcher's observations of the participants involved and is based on facts with no researcher interpretation or personal reflection. Participants' input and views must be carefully quoted.
2. Case studies typically focus on a specific person or program, where the researcher discusses characteristics or activities involved with the research subjects. In a traditional case study, the researcher will simply focus on one specific subject, whereas an ethnographer may examine the interactions of a group over a specific period of time. There are three different types of case studies including an intrinsic case study, instrumental case study, and collective case study.
3. Critical ethnographies are a specific type of ethnography in which a researcher may advocate for the group he is examining. This may be the case with minority groups or other groups that experience clear inequalities within a society.

NARRATIVE RESEARCH DESIGN

Narrative research designs collect and make available the story of an individual's life. With this design, the researcher gathers data through individual interviews, observations, or other sources. A positive aspect of this research design is the relationship or bonds developed between participants and the researcher. This bond may help researchers better understand the individuals they study as well as how to reduce potential biases or prejudices. Narrative research typically follows a chronological timeline and can be written in literary form in order to accurately provide a picture of an individual's life. Just as qualitative research designs may be, narrative research is based on subjective information and may be biased. This research design cannot serve to predict outcomes or determine cause and effects.

Characteristics of Narrative Research

1. Individual experiences are often the basis of narrative research and can provide insight into personal and social aspects of an individual's life.
2. Chronology is the timeline being examined. Maintaining a narrative in chronological order is important to gain a true feeling of the situation under examination.
3. Individual stories are told in the first person and it is the researcher's responsibility to capture all aspects of the story including predicaments, conflict, struggles, and solutions.
4. Restorying refers to the process the researcher goes through after collecting all necessary data from participants and relating the narrative. In going through this process, the researcher may also refer to previous literature in order to make casual comparisons or inferences.

Action Research Design

Action research is most common among teachers and other education professionals and involves a systematic process of gathering information in order to improve teaching methods and student learning. The basis of action research methods is to gather necessary information in order for teachers and other education professionals to reflect and improve upon their own teaching practices. This research method is conducted within the scope of the goals and objectives of the school and the school district. The process of action research consists of three stages. The first stage is identifying the necessary process to address educational issues. The second stage involves the actual educational practices of the teacher in terms of determining what is necessary to address or solve the research question. The final stage involves the teacher or teaching group to take responsibility and make the changes suggested through research findings.

Types of Action Research Design

1. Practical action research consists of identifying the problem and determining intervention based on a small scale with specific issues and goals. Practical action research is typically conducted by an individual teacher or small groups of teachers within the school or school district. Practical action research design involves reviewing teaching practices within the school or district, addressing and placing an emphasis on development, and learning for both the teacher and the student, and implementing action plans.
2. Participatory action research is a broader view of action research as this involves the school as well as communities and families. The goal of this type of research is to empower individuals and organizations in order to address problems and issues faced in the education system. Participatory action research requires the researcher to thoroughly examine societal issues, emphasize equal collaboration, and develop goals and strategies for enhancing the lives of the affected community and families.

Between-Groups Designs

Between-groups designs are used when the researcher wishes to compare two or more groups. True experiments involve random assignment of participants into either a control group or experimental group. With a true experiment, neither the participants nor the researcher knows what group participants are in, thus reducing bias and other confounding factors that may affect the results. Quasi-experiments divide participants into control and experimental groups; however, assignment is not random. This may be necessary in situations where random assignment is not possible. For example, when examining the effects of a reading intervention, a researcher may choose one third grade class of children who received the intervention as the experimental group and the other third grade class as the control group. In this situation, the researchers are unable to randomly assign students to which class they attend.

A within groups design involves examining variables and interventions within a single group. There are three main types of within group research designs. A time series design uses a baseline or pre- and post-test measures in order to collect data of one group over certain period of time. A repeated measures design examines uses each participant in a single group as its own control and experimental group. In this design, participants will receive multiple treatments over a period of time. Finally, single subject designs are an examination of a single individual. As with the time series design a baseline measurement is taken followed by an intervention; however with this design method, additional interventions may follow in which data is not collected.

Correlational Design Methods Characteristics

The display of scores of correlational design methods can be presented in a number of ways. Using a scatter plot and correlation matrices, researchers can visually depict two or more variables on a graph in order to determine the relationship between the variables.

Associations between scores help researchers to determine if there is a positive or negative correlation between two or more variables. In addition, it is important to understand that relationships are linear or nonlinear, which can be determined by arranging data visually.

Degree and strength of associations refers to the significant relationship between two variables. For example, two variables yielding a plus one correlation indicates a strong positive correlation between those two variables. Statistical analyses should be conducted in order to determine if

relationships are significant.

PMI Advantages

Differentiating Instructional Levels and Format

Teachers using a peer-mediated intervention strategy can better structure the curriculum around the needs of the students, and different levels of the curriculum can be addressed simultaneously.

Flexibility and Adaptability

Due to the nature of this intervention strategy, it is useful for students with learning disabilities, physical disabilities, and behavioral problems. Teachers can adapt the instruction to meet these needs.

Socially Valid Procedures

Research has determined PMI to be a valid intervention strategy for both the academic and social outcomes.

Cost Effectiveness and Ease of Implementation

Due to the effectiveness of PMI, students with special learning needs often do not need additional services. Additionally, PMI implements a low-tech procedure that requires little time or resources required by the school.

Availability in Prepackaged Format

There are a number of prepackaged programs for PMI including Peer Assisted Learning Strategies, which is available for both reading and math instruction.

PEER TUTORING, MONITORING, AND REPORTING

PEER TUTORING

This strategy involves dividing students into groups and providing information on tutoring methods and feedback. During each session, both students served as the tutor for a specific period of time. Students are monitored and specific skills assessed by the teacher using curriculum-based tests.

PEER MONITORING

Students are taught basic skills in observing and recording social and academic behaviors. After learning these basic skills, students observe and record the behaviors of other students as well as provide reinforcement for positive behaviors and consequences for negative behaviors.

POSITIVE PEER REPORTING

This requires students to observe, monitor, and acknowledge positive social behaviors in the classroom and school. Research has suggested that positive peer reporting increases positive peer interactions in students that have previously demonstrated socially maladaptive behavior.

RELIABILITY AND VALIDITY

Reliability refers to a tests ability to obtain the same, or very similar, score each time the test is administered. This consistency is necessary in standardized tests and those questions that do not have a high reliability must be reexamined and changed. The reliability of a test may be examined a number of ways by determining the reliability coefficient through equivalent forms, matched halves testing, or test/retest methods.

Validity refers the test's ability to actually test what it intends to test. For example, a standardized test administered to third grade students should test the various things third graders learn. A test that does not do this would be considered to have low validity.

CRITERION-RELATED VALIDITY

Criterion-related validity relies on the correlation coefficient between a score and a set criterion. This correlation coefficient is based on a +1 to -1 with 0 indicating no relationship, +1 indicating a positive relationship and -1 indicating a negative relationship. Factors that influence this type of validity include differences in test variables, for example a teacher-made assessment test versus a standardized test; differences in the criteria selected, for example, using ethnicity or attendance to assess achievement; group differences; differences in variability, or wide spans between test times or dates; and practical factors, such as gender and race.

RAW SCORE, PERCENTILE RANK, AND PERCENTAGE-CORRECT SCORE

The raw score is the initial score obtained from scoring tests. This number is typically manipulated or converted into an actual score for most standardized tests. The raw score may be based on the number of correct answers, the number of incorrect answers, or some other scoring system.

Percentile rank is a specific placement of the students' score that tells the percentage of students who scored below that student and the percentage of students who scored above that student.

Percentage-correct score is a score based on the number of correct answers divided by the total number of questions. This scoring method is typically not used with standardized testing.

Time Influence

Time influence is based on the actual time a test is given to two different groups. The time a student tests is important. For example, if a test is given at the beginning of the day or immediately after lunch, the child may be in two different mental states (i.e., alert or tired, respectively). Likewise, if a test is given at the beginning of the school year and at the end of the school year, the student may be better prepared with a more comprehensive knowledge base.

The situation-induced factor may be influenced by larger situations within the school or the community. For example, testing following a large natural disaster will affect reliability of the test.

Examinee-Incurred, Examiner-Scorer Influence, and Test Content Issues of Reliability

The examinee-incurred dimension of reliability falls on the individual taking the test and may include factors such as motivations for the test, health, or mental acuity and stamina at the time of the test.

The examiner-scorer influence dimension deals with the influence of the examiner-scorer for the test. This factor typically has little influence on objective tests but typically has more influence on subjective tests, such as a writing assessment.

Test content.deals with the actual questions of the test, which may elicit different answers when worded differently.

Standardized Testing Limitations

Standardized tests are developed and administered based on standard educational material. One major limitation of this type of testing is that they are development by commercial publishers as opposed to being developed by educators who are particularly knowledgeable of the level of information children are learning and should know. Another limitation of the use of standardized tests in schools is their use as a pass/fail measure. There are often issues with the questions on these tests as well as with scoring procedures, which may put students are an unfair disadvantage. Finally, since these tests are standard, they do not allow for individuals or cultural differences.

Educational Aims, Motivation, and Pedagogy

Active Teaching

Active teaching requires the teacher to play a significant role as leader by directing the class through the lesson. Active teaching involves effectively presenting new information, monitoring student progress, planning additional materials and situations for students to learn and apply information, and re-teaching any information students may have difficulty grasping. For teachers to be effective in active teaching, they must understand the components of planning successful lessons. These include understanding students' abilities in characteristics and matching the lesson plans to these characteristics and abilities, actively engaging students in learning tasks, monitoring progress, and most importantly, clearly outlining learning goals and expectations for the students.

Task Analysis

Task analysis activities include activities that students engage in to learn the presented materials. Teachers should consider dividing these tasks into sub tasks, especially for complicated materials. Teachers must also understand where the students are academically in order to identify beginning points for such activities. When determining task analysis activities on a large scale, such as school-wide or school district wide, teachers and administrators must determine prerequisites for lessons and activities.

Learning intentions are the goals and objectives for all task analysis activities. Learning intentions are important for teachers to stay on task and for students to understand what is expected of them academically and behaviorally in the classroom.

Types of Motivation

1. Motivational activities are activities designed to engage the learner and maintain his or her attention throughout the lesson. These activities are also designed to increase the students' interest in the material being presented.
2. Initial motivation is the beginning stage of motivating students and involves piquing their interest and curiosity of the subject being taught.
3. Within the lesson motivation is designed to maintain student interest during the lesson. This includes providing information in a way that students will understand as well creating a learning environment so the student does not feel threatened or experience fear during the learning process.
4. End of the instructional sequence motivation reinforces what was taught and provides students with a sense of achievement, which will increase motivation for the subject.

Constructivist Teaching Components

Thinking out-loud as a teaching method focuses on metacognitive skills, the ability to learn and understand. More specifically, using the thinking-out-loud approach, students begin to learn and understand what process is unnecessary for various topics. This method is particularly useful in teaching students how to proofread their own work. By requiring the students to read their work out loud, they are able to hear mistakes and begin processing strategies for proofreading.

Visualizing thinking uses visual aids, such as diagrams to think about a task. For example, students may view a diagram that depicts the specific requirements of a task thus requiring the student to think about the materials and mental efforts required to complete the task.

Paralanguage and Nonverbal Behaviors

Paralanguage are the characteristics of language that help convey a message. These characteristics include intonation, articulation, and rate of speech. Paralanguage differs between individuals and between different regions of the country. It is important to have an awareness of your paralanguage as this may affect students' ability to understand what is said and intended.

Nonverbal behaviors are gestures and body language used consciously or unconsciously when communicating. Nonverbal behaviors include eye contact, facial expressions, body posture, gestures, and general movement patterns. It is important to be aware of nonverbal behaviors in the classroom in order to ensure that these behaviors correspond with verbal communication in order to ensure clarity and understanding of what is being said.

Cooperative Learning

Cooperative learning utilizes group work in the classroom to allow students to brainstorm in completing a task. There are three types of cooperative learning: formal cooperative learning, informal cooperative learning, and cooperative groups. In cooperative learning, students understand that the success of one student means the success of all students; therefore, students are more likely to put forth their best efforts in order to help the group achieve its goals. Elements of cooperative learning are the following:

1. Establishing a goal, which include learning the material and ensuring all members of the group also learn the material.
2. Levels of cooperation, which may include a class or cooperation of the school as a whole.
3. Interaction patterns, which include students supporting each other to accomplish the goals.
4. Evaluation of outcomes, which can be assessed using criteria-referenced assessment tools to focus on the academic progress of the student and the group as a whole.

Competitive Learning

Competitive learning utilizes the notion of competition in the classroom. This may rely on motivating students to perform faster or better on a task than their peers. With competitive learning, the goal is for the individual student to perform better than his peers. Levels of competition may include the group, class, school, or nation. For example, the teacher may divide the class into groups and the groups will compete against each other to obtain the goal. Another aspect of competitive learning is this is very individualistic and students will not offer assistance to others but may attempt to interfere with their peers work in order to win the competition. In evaluating outcomes of competitive learning, norm-referenced assessment tools are used. In other words, students' work is assessed and ranked against other students' work.

Individualistic Learning

Individualistic learning is a learning method in which students work on their own in order to achieve predetermined criteria. With individualistic learning, the specific learning goals of one student may vary from the specific learning goals of another student. Levels of student work also remain at the individual level. Evaluation of outcomes is based on a criterion referenced assessment tool, which compares the student's performance on the task with a predetermined criterion, rather than the achievement of their peers. Individualistic learning relies on extrinsic motivation such as earning a good grade on the test.

Differentiated Instruction

Differentiated instruction serves to maximize learning of all students in the classroom. With this instructional method, it is understood that abilities, learning styles, and student backgrounds vary, and all require specific learning approaches. With differentiated instruction, the teacher uses a variety of teaching methods in an attempt to meet the needs of all students. This approach is important in today's classrooms because it allows teachers to increase student rate of success in the classroom, utilizes research-based best practices, increases teachers' understanding and use of assessment tools, and increases teachers' instructional strategies. It also provides teachers, administrators, and students with the tools necessary to be successful with high stakes testing and is a meaningful way to meet curriculum requirements.

Specially Designed Instruction

Specially designed instruction may include accommodations or modifications to the instructional environment in order to meet the goals of an individual education plan (IEP) for students with disabilities. Specific elements of specially designed instruction are discussed among the IEP team and determined based on the student's needs and abilities. There are two main categories for specially designed instruction including accommodations and modifications. Accommodations include changes to the instructional environment to meet the student's needs and may include increasing time allotted for time tests, allowing for more frequent breaks during tests, allowing a student to move freely around the classroom or take a bathroom break when needed, or offer the student special seating within the classroom such as in front of the class. Modifications are changes to the actual curriculum, for example modifying homework assignments.

At-Risk Learners

At-risk learners are those students whose situation or background is such that it may negatively affect their success in school. At-risk includes, but is not limited to, living with one parent, being the child of single parent, parents who failed or dropped out of high school, low socioeconomic status, living in a high growth state, poorly developed academic skills, low self-esteem, and English as a second language. It is important to note that other risk factors may come into play; however, these are the main risk factor that typically cannot be changed through intervention. When teachers and schools are aware of these risk factors and the students who may be at risk academic and behavioral interventions can be implemented in order to reduce the students the level of risk.

Minimizing Negative Effects

There are three main characteristics that a school can strive toward in order to reduce the level of risk some students may face. These include strong school leadership, school climate, and strong classroom management practices. School leadership is important for addressing risk factors of students since leaders are in the position to provide the best services possible for all students. They also can help teachers within individual classrooms provide effective instructional tools. School climate refers to the general environment of the school. Schools with positive school climate are better equipped to address the needs of at-risk students. Finally, strong classroom management practices will ensure that both the teacher and the students are fully aware of expectations, goals, and learning objectives.

The classroom and school climate is very important to student success. Overcrowding of schools may negatively affect student success and students may feel lost, or at-risk students may not be identified for being in need of intervention services. A lack of disciplinary procedures in both the school and classroom may also negatively affect success. Ineffective disciplinary procedures reduce understanding of student behavioral expectations and result in disruptions of the school or the classroom. Multicultural insensitivity is another factor, as the special needs of various cultures may not be respected or identify. Teacher and peer rejection of at-risk students may result in feelings of hopelessness as well as inhibit the students from being identified or receiving necessary services.

Involving Parents, Family, and Community

By getting the family and community involved in the education system, schools are better able to provide full services, as well as capitalize on the opinions and suggestions of families and the community. For example, when parents are involved in their student's education, they are more likely to be involved in volunteering, fund raising, and assisting with decisions related to the school such as hiring, safety, and curriculum. In addition, involved parents are also more likely to continue education at home by helping with student homework and engaging in at home learning activities. In doing this, parents and students work together as a team to increase student success. Finally, community involvement increases the feeling of ownership of the school and thus increases support.

The family structure is changing to include more than in the nuclear family, i.e., single parent families, stepfamilies, adoptions, and extended families. The structure of a student's family affects the type of support they receive, potential conflicts within the family, and the family's feeling of education.

In addition to the changing family structure, the roles of individual family members are also changing. For example, today more families have two working parents than in the past. This may result in students being left home alone after school or participating in after school programs. This may also result in reduced support and assistance for education-based activities while in the home.

The level of responsibility taken by parents and other family members has a profound effect on student success. For example, families that support each other are more likely to have successful students. On the other hand, parents or other family members who are wrapped up in personal problems may pay less attention to their school age children and increase academic risk factors.

Low-socioeconomic Status

Families living in poverty experience a number of hardships and risk factors including inadequate Health Care, housing issues, inability to provide food and clothing, and limited educational services. Students in poor health or those receiving inadequate rest and nutrition go to school unprepared for learning. Students living in poverty also often attend financially struggling schools that have few resources for students as well as poorly prepared teachers. General characteristics of low socioeconomic students include their being older than their same grade peers, having a higher drop-out rate, and being less likely to obtain gainful employment. Likewise, these students are also more likely to have health issues, which affect their ability to attend school on a regular basis

Wrap-around Services

Wraparound services utilize sources from the school and community in order to provide at-risk students with as much support as possible. For example, in addition to providing student services within the school, community resource agencies may provide the students with a social worker in order to address needs for nutrition, clothing, or counseling. Wrap-around services are beneficial to not only the student but the family, and may help increase family participation and support in the student's education.

ESL CLASSROOMS

1. Self-contained ESL classrooms -

   These classrooms contain only students with English as a second language for all core subjects. Students in self-contained ESL classrooms have the opportunity to interact and work with non ESL students for music, art, and physical education, as well as in the library.

2. Integrated 50/50 ESL classrooms -

   These classrooms contain equal numbers of ESL and non ESL students and focus on cooperative learning methods, role models, hands on activities, demonstrations, and modeling in order to improve the English language skills of the ESL students.

3. Integrated group classrooms -

   These classrooms are typically used in schools with few ESL students. Within an integrated group classroom, ESL instructional methods will be applied as appropriate.

HIGH STAKES TESTING

High-stakes testing is the use of standardized tests in order to determine achievement and make major educational decisions. High-stakes testing has become a hallmark of schools since the No Child Left Behind Act. Examples of this include high school exit exams and test scores to determine promotion to the next grade. The notion of high stakes testing suggests that a single measure is used in making these decisions rather than a comprehensive assessment of a student's ability. Benefits of standardized testing such as those used in high stakes testing include general assessment of the student's achievement as well as assessment of the teacher. However, downfalls to this type of testing include increased stress on the students, teachers, and administrators as well as the possibility of being held back academically.

RETENTION

Retention refers to being held back or repeating a grade. This is the result of academic failure to meet predetermined criteria for promotion. Retention is more common in males and minorities including African Americans and Hispanics. Students who are retained are often young for their age and have significant developmental delays. They also have attention, behavioral, or emotional problems. Often, the students are English language learners and demonstrate difficulties reading. From a social aspect, retained students often tend to live in poverty, in single parent families, and do not have positive educational support at home. Students in grades first through third are most likely to be retained, often due to poor reading skills. While this retention may be beneficial at first, there is no indication that there are long-term benefits for retaining a student at this level. Likewise, students retained during the middle school years often demonstrate negative behaviors and attitudes toward academics. Students retained in high school are a significant predictor of dropout.

MULTI-TIERED INSTRUCTIONAL PROGRAMS

Multi-tiered instructional programs utilize differentiated instruction across tiers in order to meet specific student needs. Within this instructional strategy, teachers will spend time determining student skills, utilize grouping of the students to maximize learning time and time on task, and allow opportunities for additional learning or instruction, as necessary. Within this approach, students needing additional assistance will have the opportunity to receive secondary intervention, as the need for this level of intervention is determined by screening, progress monitoring, and interventions focused on practice and the feedback. Often, the secondary intervention can be effective when provided for fifteen to thirty minutes daily. Tertiary intervention may be necessary if a student continues to struggle after receiving secondary intervention services. This level of intervention is customized to a student's abilities and needs, and is comprehensive in nature.

Supplemental Reading Instruction

The planning process is an important step in writing and students may need additional assistance including reading prompts, assistance with decision-making and problem solving, and developing complex sophisticated writing plans.

Writing production involves writing to communicate. In order to assist students in writing production, instructional and motivational strategies, including constructive feedback, may be necessary. In addition, setting aside writing time, typically between twenty-five and thirty-five minutes a day, is necessary for students to gain adequate practice for this task. Students with learning disabilities may need additional time to practice.

The process of revising written work is an important learning tool. Revisions will occur at various levels including content, grammar, punctuation, and spelling. Developing effective revision strategies include requiring students to read their read work out loud and obtain peer feedback.

Text Structure Instruction

Text structure instruction is a method of planning in order to improve students' ability to brainstorm and logically develop in written story. This instructional method uses cues to help students develop logical connections between written text and illustrations. Specifically, students learn to identify story elements, such as characters, setting, time, ending, and character reactions. Learning this information is accomplished by reviewing and analyzing previous stories. In terms of developing logical stories, students learn through modeling, guidance, prompting, and direct questioning. Text structure instruction is enhanced through practice and feedback. Some research suggests that students learning through the text structure instruction method are able to develop complex, goal oriented, and logical stories.

Direct Instruction in Writing Mechanics

Using direct instruction allows the teacher to develop writing lessons that are based on systematic steps that correspond to the developmental writing stages as well as provide immediate feedback. For example, the teacher may begin the lesson by modeling proper writing mechanics and implement group work to support information development. Finally, the teacher may test the class on what was presented during the lesson. Because direct instruction involves the active interaction between teachers and students, this teaching method is effective for students with behavioral problems and learning disabilities. One such program that uses direct instruction is the Reasoning and Writing program, which focuses on a variety of writing genres including essays, expository statements, and narratives. A downside of direct instruction in teaching reading mechanics is necessary intervention that may be required above and beyond regular instruction. Due to the comprehensiveness of this teaching method, lessons are typically 50 minutes along and do not allow for additional intervention time.

Direct Spelling Instruction

Teachers may employ various methods for spelling instruction including phonemic, whole word, and morphemic approaches. Phonemic approaches focus on teaching students the sounds that correspond with single letters in groups of letters. The whole word spelling approach focuses on site words and memorization. With both the phonemic and whole word approach to spelling instruction, students will review the word, write the word, and repeat this process if necessary. The morphemic approach to spelling instruction involves teaching students the rules of spelling such as prefixes, suffixes, and roots of words. When deciding on a specific approach for spelling instruction, educators must understand that not all approaches will be effective for all students and they must understand the specific learning needs of the class in order to develop an appropriate approach.

PMI

Promoting active engagement The use of PMI strategies increases the active engagement of all students as well as opportunity to ask questions, and provide and receive feedback. Active engagement is successful with students with learning disabilities and behavioral problems since individualized attention can be given.

Improving academic performance outcomes With the PMI strategy, students can engage in peer reading and other collaborative activities such as tutoring to increase performance an understanding of material.

Improving peer interactions in classroom climate The PMI strategy requires that students work together thus increasing peer interactions and opportunities for cooperative learning. Another benefit of this strategy is peer modeling of positive behaviors and academic success.

Encourage student autonomy Using this strategy, students develop their own academic goals and monitor their own academic success. This places accountability on the students as well as increases their motivation for learning and feelings of independence.

Parent-Teacher Cooperation

School age children spend about equal amounts of weekday time at school and at home. It is important for parents and teachers to help each other reinforce positive behaviors. Schools can promote this interaction by encouraging positive behaviors and encouraging parents to visit the school. Parent and teacher communication is also critical and can be accomplished through notes home to parents, and parent-teacher conferences. While it is important that both parents and teachers help reinforce positive social behaviors, it is unnecessary and inappropriate to attempt to tell a parent how to raise the child. However, teachers and schools can provide information on positive parenting techniques and other behavior modification strategies that may be used in the school.

TDI

A Typical Day Interview (TDI) is often conducted with the parent and involves discussing the child's typical day activities. In discussing a typical day, the psychologist may be able to identify factors or antecedents to problem behaviors. Parents are prompted to discuss specific activities, state their reactions, and discuss outcomes. Additionally, the psychologist will be able to determine negative parental reactions to problem behaviors. These interview questions typically focus first on bedtime and then chronologically to events through the next day and focus on the child-parent interactions when conflicts are likely to occur. Parent and child expectations of behavior are identified and the information can be used for future functional behavioral assessments and interventions.

Safe and Responsive Schools Program

The Safe and Responsive Schools Program is an alternative to zero tolerance policies often seen in many schools. This program encourages positive long-term outcomes rather than the short-term outcomes seen with zero-tolerance policies. School teams work together to develop a positive social curriculum that outlines student expectations with regard to social interactions and positive behaviors. With the Safe and Responsive Schools Program, schools strategically create a positive school climate and promote teaching alternative methods of dealing with conflicts. Schools implement early identification and intervention systems in order to identify and assist at-risk students (both behavioral and academic). Finally, this program encourages schools to develop and implement positive interventions for students who demonstrate persistent behavior problems.

Consulting

Consulting is the process by which one professional refers to another professional about a case or situation. As a school psychologist, this may involve being the consultant or consulting with another mental health professional about a student. The consulting relationship is triadic due to the cooperation of three parties: the consultee, the consultant, and the client. The relationship is developed in order to solve a specific goal. For example, a school psychologist may consult with another mental health professional about a student with a severe behavioral problem. In the process of this relationship, two things will typically occur: a solution is developed for the problem at hand and the consultee expands his or her knowledge base on a particular problem.

Consulting Characteristics

1. The consultant is an indirect services provider to the client. This is so because the consultant will typically only meet with the consultee, not the client.
2. Consultants may be internal or external. Within the school environment, an internal consultant may be another school psychologist or counselor within the same school or district. An external consultant may include a private practice psychiatrist. In general, the consultant relationship is voluntary when consulting from one professional to another; no fees are collected for consulting.
3. This relationship is strictly professional and does not deal with personal concerns of the consultee.
4. This relationship maintains a collaborative environment in that both the consultant and consultee work together to find solutions.
5. Consulting is formal and organized with a defined problem and goals.

Mental Health Consultation Model

When discussing the mental health model of consultation, it is important to understand that the consultant is the mental health expert often called to consult on or to directly diagnose a mental health issue. Conversely, the consultee may be a professional or non professional who administers the treatment based on the expert's diagnosis. There are four main approaches to this type of consultation, including client-centered, consultee-centered, program-centered, and consultee-centered administration. In the client-centered form, the consultant will assess the case and help the consultee develop an appropriate treatment plan. In the consultee-centered form, the consultant focuses on increasing the knowledge of the consultee. In the program-centered form, the consultant may focus on developing or enhancing a specific treatment program to be administered by other professionals or non-professionals. Finally, in the consultee-centered administrative form, the consultant focuses on the functions of the consultee's job; in other words, the consultant helps the consultee do the job more effectively (e.g., taking effective case notes or completing the proper informed consent forms).

Behavioral Consultation Model

The behavioral consultation model of the consultation process is rooted in well-structured theories of human behavior. Using this model, the consultant and consultee gather information concerning a problem, and then develop goals and methods for solving that problem. Similar to other behavioral approaches, the behavioral consultation model follows six steps including identifying the problem, analyzing the problem, choosing a target behavior, developing objectives, developing and implementing an intervention, and evaluating the behavior. This model is typically used when the consultee is having problems with a specific case; the consultant and consultee work together to provide the client the best possible care.

Consulting Children

There are eight functions of consultation for the school psychologist. First, consultations may come in the form of developing and conducting professional development classes or lectures in order to openly discuss issues related to school children. Consultation will also be used to assist teachers with addressing specific behavioral issues. School psychologists may also simply provide teachers with information or materials concerning behavioral or academic issues. Consultants may expand into the community by participating in community organizations or boards aimed at addressing issues the children in the community face or by developing and conducting parenting classes. Finally, school psychologists consult with administrators, teachers, or other health care professionals in providing guidance, information, or interpreting test results.

Process Consultation Model

Process consultation is focused on assisting the consultee in better understanding a topic or situation by exploring six topic areas. These six topic areas include increasing communication skills; problem solving and decision-making skills; group roles, cooperation, and competition; leadership; and various group processes, such as the development, growth, and norms of a group. During the consulting process, it is the consultant's role to help the consultee understand these processes and serve to facilitate in individual and group sessions until the consultee is comfortable with the various skills and strategies necessary to be effective.

Multicultural Consultation Model

The multicultural consultation model takes culture into consideration, specifically stressing cultural understanding from the consultant. Using this consulting model, the consultant focuses on multicultural issues and strengths in order to help the consultee to be aware of these issues and use the strengths in his or her own work. Various factors play a role in the multicultural consultation model, which include trust, diversity, learning to avoid jargon, and being cognizant of how others perceive and interpret the actions and information provided by the consultant. When taking this consultation viewpoint, it is important that the consultant provide support for both the consultee and the client, provide cross-cultural learning opportunities, strive to increase confidence, and enhance the consultee's knowledge and therapeutic skills.

Consultation Process

Preentry

The potential consultant will determine if he is fit to consult. This may include introspection or asking various questions to determine if he has the knowledge, skills, and leadership abilities to be an effective consultant.

Entry, Problem Exploration, and Contracting

This is the beginning of the actual consulting process. During this stage, the consultant will gather all necessary information in order to determine the problem and begin formulating a solution or strategy to address the problem.

Information Gathering, Problem Confirmation, and Goal Setting

During this stage, the consultant may gather qualitative and quantitative data in order to better assess the problem and set achievable goals.

Collaborative Relationships

Collaborative relationships typically include five key actions. First, members of a collaboration must come together. As individuals must understand what others may bring to a situation to achieve a goal and, in coming together, all parties commit to working together to meet the goals of the collaboration. Next, the collaboration must have a shared vision. Since this process involves working with others, it is essential that all involved understand the issues or goals and are willing to share their knowledge and resources with the others. Then, developing a plan of action is the next activity followed by implementing the plan. Finally, as with other processes, it is necessary to evaluate or assess the plan to determine its effectiveness.

Collaboration and School Psychologist

Collaboration is a coordinated interaction between two professionals with the goal of completing a task. Both parties involved understand that the relationship is voluntary and is often considered a partnership. In a collaborative relationship, several characteristics emerge including equal voice, mutual goals, shared responsibility, and shared resources. Collaborations may be formal or informal; however, all collaborations have shared goals, values, and activities to achieve those goals. Collaborations are a key component to a successful school psychologist; it is necessary to work with other professionals, teachers, parents, and members of the community in order to evaluate problems on an individual and school-wide level, and then develop and assess interventions.

Collaboration and Consultation

There are similarities between collaboration and consultation. Both address a problem or issue that is too complex for only one individual to handle. Additionally, both processes involve the combined efforts of two or more professionals, whether they are in the same profession or not. Finally, both processes rely on common goals, developing plans to achieve those goals, and assessing those goals to either end the relationship when the goals are met or to redefine the interventions to better meet unmet goals. In terms of differences, a collaboration is a partnership and all parties are considered equal; whereas in a consultative relationship, the consultant is typically the more knowledgeable of the pair and attempts to share that knowledge with the consultee.

Teamwork

Teams are groups of two or more individuals working together to achieve the same goal. A common team in the school setting is the team created to develop a student's individual education plan (IEP). Teams may consist of professionals, teachers, students, and parents. When developing a team, one must clearly define the goals and objectives of the team as well as individual roles. Team members must also understand that there is typically a growth process as the team begins to work together. The school psychologist will work in teams in order to provide full services and support to students as well as to develop various programs and curriculum for the school or the community.

Team Characteristics

Effective teams demonstrate the following characteristics:

1. All members of the team trust that the other members will do their part and they respect what each member brings to the team.
2. Team members are able to implement positive problem solving and conflict resolution techniques in order to work through problems or conflicts during their time together.

3. There is accountability of all team members to complete their assigned duties to the best of their ability.
4. Members offer each other support and encouragement as well as help other members when necessary.

Johnson and Johnson's Guidelines for Effective Teams

Johnson and Johnson developed the following guidelines for teams:

1. Teams must be encouraged to develop and clearly define their mission, goals, and objectives.
2. Teams must meet or interact on a regular basis.
3. The team must have clearly defined rules of conduct which all members follow.
4. Team and individual progress must be measured and assessed on a regular basis.
5. Teams must assess how they are moving forward to meet their goals.
6. In situations where there is no or little movement to meet goals, the team must reassess their methods and determine another strategy to meet their stated goals.
7. Teams should offer or engage in training when necessary.
8. Team members must acknowledge the success of each member within the group.

Role Shift

Role shift is a consultation method aimed to help the consultee acknowledge what methods have worked with clients and, more importantly, what methods have not worked with their clients. Using this technique, the consultant will have the consultee list the various methods they have implemented during the counseling session. From there, both the consultant and the consultee review the list and determine which methods were effective. The consultee will then keep the list of both effective and ineffective methods handy as a reference guide. This guide will remind the consultee of how to respond to the client's various behaviors in order to make the session more effective.

Logical consequences

Logical consequences is a technique used to teach children the consequences of a behavior rather than punishing the child for the behavior. Using this technique serves various purposes. First, the child learns the rules of society because he is required to face the logical consequence of his or her actions. For example, if a child destroys the playroom, a traditional punishment may be to have the child sit in time out. On the other hand, a logical consequence would be to require the child to clean the playroom. This activity teaches the child that if he dirties or destroys something, he will be made to fix or clean it. Using this method, parents and teachers still maintain healthy authority.

Combining Teamwork, Consultations, and Collaboration

Teamwork, consultations, and collaboration all focus on achieving a specific and agreed upon goal. The benefits of working together include relying on the various knowledge bases and resources of each member in the group and dividing large projects among many individuals. Using these three methods together can benefit all involved as well as assist in meeting the goals quicker or more effectively. For example, a team may seek a consultant to educate the team on matters beyond the collective expertise of the group. Additionally, one team may collaborate with another team in order to meet goals in different geographic regions. For example, a curriculum development team in District A may collaborate with a curriculum development team in District B.

Evaluation of a Consultative Relationship

When assessing the consultative relationship, the consultant will observe the following:

1. General appearance, behavior, and attitude of the client. This may include dress, cleanliness, facial expressions, and other body language of the client.
2. Observation of speech and thought processes of the client. This information is gathered by engaging the client in conversation and listening for delays in speech, logic, and completeness of the client's thoughts, and long pauses or silences as the client speaks.
3. Emotional status and reactions of the client are an important assessment observation, as inconsistencies in these processes may indicate various disorders or dysfunctions.
4. Orientation and awareness of the client. It is important for the consultant to assess if the client is aware of his surroundings and aware of why he in the therapy session.

Family Emotional Processes

Emotional processes of families are typically generational. In other words, the children learn emotional processes from their parents and will eventually pass on these processes, whether positive or negative, to their own children. This cycle continues unless it is broken by some means, as often occurs in therapy. Depending on the emotional stability of the parents, the children in the family will either follow the parents' emotions or will attempt to detach themselves, or become undifferentiated. Often when detaching themselves from the family, children maintain negative emotional processes into adulthood regardless. As a therapist, being aware of the cyclic property of family emotions is beneficial in addressing and changing the negative processes within the family.

The function of emotional process within the family works similarly to those present in society as a whole. Often those individuals who detach themselves from their family's dysfunctional emotional processes become undifferentiated from the family as well as future relationships. This is also seen with individuals who detach themselves from society. Additionally, in both families and society, these processes are seen generationally and can only be broken through specific interventions. Of note, in both families and larger social groups, individuals or groups of people who detach themselves from the larger group tend to overreact and are more emotional than those who remain a part of the family or society.

Structural Family Therapy

Within structural family therapy, the therapist considers each member of the family as a fully functioning member. As such, each individual is neither the sole initiator nor the sole cause to the problems and issues discussed in the therapeutic environment. Likewise, changes in one individual cannot solve the problems of the family; therefore, the therapist works with the family to change the entire structure of the family. Additionally, this method of therapy relies on the fact that there is a specific organization and hierarchy of the family, which must also be respected.

Strategic Family Therapy

Strategic family therapy is brief, approximately 10 sessions. The underlying theory behind this form of therapy is the notion that behaviors displayed in the family are within a set context of that particular family. For example, members of families with ineffective problem solving techniques may display behavioral problems associated with their ineffective problem solving. It is the therapist's job to identify these dysfunctional behavioral patterns and provide the family with information in correcting them. As such, this form of therapy is solution and results focused. Strategic family therapy aims to understand the family's unique structure and change the maladaptive factors of the structure into positive factors in order to increase family communication and cohesiveness.

FAMILY COUNSELING

Family therapy is a dynamic approach to counseling as families varies so vastly. However, when applying the systems approach to family counseling, it is important for the therapist to consider and be aware of the following factors:

1. The spousal relationship. This relationship may affect the family as a whole and it is important to understand how spouses work together as well as apart.
2. Differentiation of self. This concept relates to how members of the family see themselves as individuals.
3. Triangles. These occur when two members enlist a third member during a conflict.
4. Emotional processes relate to how the family, as a whole, handles stress and conflict.
5. Family projection is how the parents pass different behaviors, both good and bad, onto their children.
6. Multigenerational transmission process. Like family projection, this factor deals with how social traits or behaviors are passed on from one generation to the next.

SALVADOR MINUCHIN

Minuchin recognized the importance of developing and maintaining a relationship with the family as a whole. As such, he proposed three methods of developing this relationship. First, the therapist should engage in tracking. This is a way to show interest in the family as well as to learn about the family. The second method is mimicry. This method requires the therapist to adopt a communication style similar to that of the family. Finally, the therapist offers support for the family's issues by accepting the issue or problem and by helping the family solve the problem. Minuchin stated once the relationship is developed, other factors must be considered. These include determining the roles and responsibilities of each family member, how the family makes decisions, and how the family views and respects privacy.

MILTON ERIKSON

Erikson believed in client centered therapy and developed three main principles to approaching family therapy. First, he believed that it is important to understand and respect the client's reality and use this one, rather than conventional reality or that of the therapist, to structure the therapeutic sessions. Second, Erikson felt that therapy was an active process and both the client and therapist had to actively pursue the goals and objectives of the therapy. Finally, in order to make changes within the family system, the targeted individual must make changes in his or her personal life.

JOHN GORRMAN

The focus of John Gorrman's behavioral interview method is to increase awareness of the family on factors causing the dysfunction. During Stage 1 of this method, the therapist encourages the family to discuss why they decided to seek therapy. This discussion allows the therapist to better understand the dynamics of the family. During Stage 2, specific goals are developed for each family member and the therapist encourages a discussion for why the clients choose those goals to work on. Stage 3 involves creating checklists of various issues and discussing why the client included the items and possible solutions for resolving those items. In Stage 5, the therapist provides the family with strategies to resolve problems and the clients are tasked with practicing these strategies at home. During Stage 5, the family reports back to the therapist on how the strategies were used and includes the responses received from the other family members. Finally, during Stage 6, the therapy concludes and a contract is created for the family to continue working toward their individual goals.

Paradoxical Interventions

Paradoxical interventions play on the client's unwillingness to participate in therapy to change his or her behaviors. In such interventions, the therapist will encourage the client to continue the maladaptive behaviors and, in the case of children, will encourage the parents to play along. For example, a child who displays tantrums will be encouraged to continue the tantrums; however, he will be instructed to have them only during certain points of the day. Throughout the intervention period, the client will begin to gain insight into the maladaptive behavior and will cease the behavior. Paradoxical interventions may also include stressing the positive traits or accomplishments of a client despite their dysfunction or maladaptive behavior.

Family Therapy Interview

Stage I

The social stage - During this stage, the therapist develops a relationship with the client, learns common behavioral patterns of the family, and begins developing goals for future sessions.

Stage II

The problem stage - This is where the specific problem or problems of the family are defined and discussed.

Stage III

The interaction stage - During the interaction stage, the problem is discussed further with a focus on the family interacting with one another in an effort to increase communication and identify family roles associated with the problem.

Stage IV

The goal setting stage - Specific goals for addressing and resolving the problem are developed.

Virginia Satir

Virginia Satir's conjoint family therapy method combines family therapy with the notions of Gestalt concepts in that the whole is the sum of its parts. Likewise, Satir identified that what outsiders see when looking at a family is actually only 10 percent of what is actually going on in that family. In working with families, Satir focused on increasing the family's understanding of commitment, expression, the freedom to agree or disagree with each other, and the ability to ask each other questions or for clarification. Additionally, she emphasized the fact that families must trust and rely on each other.

Placater, Blamer, Computer, Distracter, and Leveler

Placater

The placater typically remains calm at all times and attempts to mend family relationships and stop arguments among other family members.

Blamer

The blamer is often bossy or acts a director of the family. These individuals often have low self-esteem and use blaming others as a defense mechanism.

Computer

The computer is typically quiet, rarely displays his or her feelings, is logical, and is often correct. He may have low self-esteem and use intelligence as a defense mechanism to cover up his or her insecurities.

Distractor

The distractor is likely dishonest and tends to change the subject, especially when the subject is of a sensitive matter.

Leveler

The leveler is honest and true to his or her feelings.

NASP

The National Association of School Psychologists (NASP) developed the Principles for Professional Ethics to protect students' well-being. In addition, these established ethics also serve to protect teachers, school administrators, parents, and other interested parties, such as school staff and interns. The Principles for Professional Ethics covers a range of issues including rights of the school, student, and communities; assessments and intervention; data collection and reporting; relationship between shareholders; and the use of various materials for research and publication. In covering these, as well as other related topics, these ethics serve as a guideline for school psychologists (working both in schools and in the community) to provide safe and effective services to students, schools, and the community.

APA's Ethical Principles of Psychologists

The American Psychological Association's Ethical Principles of Psychologists and Code of Conduct covers a range of psychological subfields. Within these principles and codes are general principles (goals) and ethical standards (enforceable rules for conduct). General principles include beneficence and nonmalfeasance, fidelity and responsibility, integrity, justice, and respect for people's rights and dignity. These principles are to be used as guidelines when determining the ethically responsible response to various satiations. The APA's ethical standards include revolving ethical issues, competence, human relations, privacy and confidentiality, advertising and other public statements, and record keeping and fees. These ethical standards serve as a means to ensure ethics are upheld. Failure to uphold these standards may result in disciplinary action.

Ethical Absolutism and Relativism

Ethical absolutism is the belief in a concrete, absolute universal moral or ethical truth. In other words, there are morals that apply to all humans and are not culturally or time-dependent. With ethical absolutism, there is no consideration for specific factors of a situation when determining if an action is right or wrong.

Ethical relativism suggests that morals are cultural and time-dependent. This notion places the emphasis of an ethical action on the specific situation or individual. For example, something may be right for one individual but not another. What is right will depend on a combination of all the factors involved.

Twentieth Century Developments

The beginning of the twentieth century was met with changing needs of the public and a rapidly changing educational system. Compulsory education, regulations on child labor laws, new social structures resulting from reconstruction, new educational tools, and the emergence of psychology in general in the United States, all served to offer the opportunity and need for the field of school psychology. Additionally, it was during this time that IQ was introduced as a means to assess student's abilities and, socially, racial segregation was a common practice. These two factors enhanced the need for special support services in the schools.

WELLNESS MODEL

The wellness model views mental health on a continuum with mentally healthy individuals at one end and mentally unhealthy individuals at the other end. In addition, this model includes scales of wellness in all aspects of the individual's life. Using this model, the therapist will assess the client and determine where he lies on the continuum as well as their level of functioning in various areas of their life and, from there, determine to best possible treatment plan. The therapist will also work with the client in order to incorporate the client's goals for treatment and his own mental health.

PRIVACY AND CONFIDENTIALITY

Privacy and confidentiality, with respect to the school psychologist-student relationship, refers to maintaining a safe counseling environment where the student's privacy is maintained. Privacy refers to the immediate surroundings. For the school psychologist, this means that all sessions with students are conducted away from other students and teachers in a quiet location where the student and therapist are free to talk without being overheard. Confidentiality extends beyond the session and refers to the promise the therapist makes with the client that things discussed during a session will not be repeated.

ETHICS, MORALS, AND LAW

Ethics is a philosophical study of appropriate human behaviors, which is based on the morals of a society. These behaviors guide professionals in developing laws and guidelines for treating and respecting the privacy of their clients.

Morals are broad generalizations for how to act in society. Morals may change based on the particular society as well as the time an individual lives. However, general human morals tend to govern most individuals in current society.

Laws are formally enacted morals and most often voted into legislation. When broken, laws come with a penalty of some sort, often in the form of a fine or imprisonment.

SLIPPERY SLOPE PHENOMENON

The slippery slope phenomenon occurs the first time a professional acts unethically. This may even include a situation where a professional is aware of unethical practices but takes no actions. Philosophically, the slippery slope is one in which, once a professional begins down the slope or acts unethically, they will continue to slip downward or act unethically. In order to avoid the slippery slope phenomenon, a professional may seek external support systems in order to maintain accountability in their own practice. This additional support system will also provide the professional with sources for professional development.

SIX-PRINCIPLES FOR ETHICS

1. Respect of autonomy refers to the therapist's ability to allow the client to choose his or her own direction in life. It is not the responsibility of the therapist to dictate how the client lives, but to help teach the necessary skills for living a healthy life.
2. Nonmaleficence refers to unintentionally causing harm to the client.
3. Beneficence, which is the opposite of nonmaleficence, means that the therapist will do everything they can to help the client.
4. Justice is the professional's obligation to uphold the ethics and laws of the profession.
5. Fidelity is taking responsibility and being accountable for maintaining professionalism in the relationship.
6. Veracity is remaining truthful with the client.

ETHICAL DECISION-MAKING PROCESS

Some situations may not have clearly defined guidelines or laws. Therefore, it is necessary to first clearly identify the suspected problem. Next, consider the moral principles of in the specific context of the problem. Then, tune into one's feelings. Personal emotions often affect professional judgment; therefore, understanding emotions will help in the ethical decision making process. Consult with colleagues, which can help in determining all the possible options as well as consequences for certain actions. Involve the client in the decision-making process. Since many therapeutic related decisions most likely involve a situation with a client, it is thus necessary to discuss the situation with the client. Finally, identify desired outcomes and consider actions. In doing so, the therapist may be able to determine or even eliminate different actions.

MODEL FOR PROFESSIONAL PRACTICE

The first building block is intentionality, or having good intentions when treating clients. In the helping profession, there is often no absolute rule for helping; therefore, the practitioner must enter each session or professional relationship with the intention to provide the best care possible. Next, is upholding the moral principles of the helping profession, which are a set of principles based on group consensus and ethical guidelines. The third building block is an understanding or knowledge of the laws that govern the profession. The fourth building block of this model is the courage of one's convictions, or the confidence that one is working with good intentions and with the knowledge of the laws, morals, and ethics surrounding the profession.

VIRTUE ETHICS

1. Integrity. Therapists maintain their integrity by helping because it is right and ethical. This may specifically come into play in situations where the case is beyond the scope of practice for the therapist. In order to maintain integrity, the therapist may consult with another professional and thus offer the client the best possible care.
2. Discernment refers to the ability to understand a situation and make an ethical, effective decision.
3. Acceptance of emotion. It is necessary for the therapist to understand his own emotions and emotional limits in order to avoid becoming emotional involved or burned out.
4. Self-awareness refers to knowing oneself.
5. Interdependence with the community refers to the understanding that everything is affected by the context of the environment and the community in which one lives.

SELF TESTS TO REAFFIRM AN ETHICAL DECISION

1. The test of justice. In this self-test, the therapist asks himself if he would have made the same decision had different individuals been involved. In other words, was the decision made based on some personal bias toward or against the individuals involved?
2. The test of universality. In this test, the therapist asks himself if he would recommend the decision to a colleague in the same situation.
3. The test of publicity. In this test, the therapist asks himself if he would feel comfortable if the decision was made public.
4. The final test is moral traces. In other words, the therapist determines their feelings about their decision, or decides if they have doubts about their decision.

DIFFERENT CREDENTIALS

A degree is the university educational level obtained by the therapist. This education will have come from an accredited university and will be at the master's or doctoral level.

State licenses are the state's recognition that an individual has earned the appropriate education and is knowledgeable in the foundations, practice, and laws of the profession. States licenses typically require a comprehensive testing component.

Like the state licenses, a national voluntary certification is a professional certification to demonstrate mastery in the profession. This certification validates the individual has obtained the appropriate education and has taken the nationally administered test.

Most schools require only an advanced university degree and a state license to practice.

Fair and Just Psychologist

According to the National Association of School Psychologists' code of ethics, it is the responsibility of the school psychologist to create an environment that is inviting and safe. Additionally, the psychologist should strive to maintain this environment throughout the school. Specifically, psychologists will not allow practices that are discriminatory and they should be culturally aware. Also, psychologists should serve as advocates for students who may be treated unfairly and work with the school to change any policies, procedures, or social climates that promote unfair treatment. Finally, the school psychologist should ensure that all students have equal opportunities to participate in or receive necessary services offered by the school and the community.

HIPAA

The Health Insurance Portability and Accountability Act (HIPAA) is an administrative function of handling client records and confidential health insurance information. The purpose of this act is to ensure confidentiality of these records is maintained and the client's privacy is upheld. Since the advent of electronic records, concerns have been raised regarding the safety of medical records, and this act requires that all electronic records are standardized and contain unique patient identification numbers. In addition to the guidelines set forth for practitioners, HIPAA also contains guidelines for patients in terms of obtaining copies of their personal records.

Comprehensive and Integrated School Psychological Services

The Model for Comprehensive and Integrated School Psychological Services was developed by the National Association of School Psychologists. The purpose of this model is to offer school psychologist a set of guidelines in order to provide psychological services at the community, state, and federal levels. Included in this model is information for all shareholders such as teachers, administrators, and other community services in order to work together in providing these services. There are ten domains included in this model including information about the foundations of psychology and education, strategies and skills for serving students, ability to maintain a safe environment, and understanding of professional responsibilities.

School Psychologist Competences

1. The school psychologist must understand their own scope of practice. In other words, the school psychologist is responsible for referring a case or client or seeking consultation services when there is a situation beyond his knowledge and understanding.
2. School psychologists may not embellish their academic or professional achievements.
3. School psychologists must maintain current knowledge of the profession. This is accomplished by attending professional development courses and continuing education.
4. School psychologists must not invite conflict but make attempts to resolve conflict. This is particularly important when the conflict involves the school, community, parents, or a combination of these elements.

Education of All Handicapped Children Act

Public Law 94–142: Education of All Handicapped Children Act, passed in 1975, was one of the first acts implemented in the United States that requires public schools to provide special education services to those students in need. Under this law, all schools are required to identify students with learning disabilities. Disabilities that are the result of environment, cultural, or socioeconomic status are not included and do not require intervention services that would fall under special education. Therefore, only students with congenital physical or mental disabilities or those caused from trauma qualify for special education services. Over the years, legislators have recognized the need to expand the definition of disability and have thus amended this act.

IDEA 97

Public Law 105-17: Individuals with Disabilities Education Act (IDEA 97) was a revision of the Education of All Handicapped Children Act. This revision was necessary due to a continual inappropriate labeling and identification of students with disabilities within the public education system. Specifically, many minority children were being mislabeled as students with disabilities, thus resulting in a highly disproportionate number of minority children in special education services. Specifically, this act stated that a child could not be identified as having a disability solely on insufficient instruction in reading, math, or English proficiency. Additionally, this act requires public schools to collect demographic data including ethnicity, to determine where large discrepancies occur in special education programs, as well as address these discrepancies.

Scope

The scope of the school psychologist includes all duties aimed at improving the emotional, mental, and academic health of the students. This scope follows a continuum of services including ensuring all students receive effective classroom instruction, working with teachers and administrators to provide additional instruction to students in need, and advocating and providing for students who need crisis management services. The health, safety, and success of every student must be the priority of the school psychologist and, therefore, the psychologist needs to understand his or her limits and seek consultation when necessary.

Utilitarianism and Deontology

Utilitarianism, or consequential ethics, is based on the notion of the greater good. Believers of utilitarianism most likely would act to positively affect as many people as possible. Utilitarianism can also be considered consequentialism, since the focus of the moral act is on the result, not the act itself.

Deontology relies to the notion that an action or behavior is required simply because it is ethically right, regardless of the consequences to the larger public.

IDEA, 2004

Public Law 108-446: Individuals with Disabilities Education Improvement Act (IDEA 2004) was a further revision of the laws dealing with students with disabilities, specifically in terms of race and ethnicity. IDEA 2004 requires public schools to identify students with disabilities including collecting information regarding race and ethnicity. Schools are also required to identify disabilities and address any discrepancies that may occur in special education. Additionally, IDEA 2004 has included technical assistance, demonstration projects, information dissemination, and implementation of research-based program evaluations for special education and public schools. This goal of the revised law is to provide students with disabilities all the services possible and to allow these students the same opportunities as those without disabilities. In order to ensure that all public schools adhere to this law, federal funding may be revoked or suspended if schools are found in noncompliance.

Professionalism and Best Practices

Professionalism is typically based on guidelines of a profession as well as personal principles of how to conduct oneself in the work place. This will include an individual's dress, the language he uses at work, and his personality toward clients and colleagues, as well as professional competences.

Best practices are those practices that have been shown to provide or offer the best possible services to the clients. Best practices are often proposed based on empirical research. While professionals are not required to follow best practices, they are recommended as they represent positive professionalism and provide guidelines for following other ethical and legal components of the profession.

Scientific and Humanistic

Those psychologists who view psychology with a scientific eye often also use the medical model to diagnosis and treat. These professionals view symptoms and treatment outcomes. The scientific culture tends to favor quantitative research and the notion that there are fixed variables that determine human behavior. The scientific side of psychology takes place most often in the laboratory, where objective observations and measurements can be controlled. On the other hand, the humanistic culture of psychology sees human behavior as an ever changing construct that is determined by the individual's environment and society. This culture of psychology tends toward qualitative research and more subjective experiences. The humanistic culture of psychology takes place in the field.

Today's School

There is an increasing awareness and move toward serving students with disabilities; this will place this emphasis on the school psychologist. Therefore, school psychologists must be aware of the changing education legislation as well as developing innovative education and intervention strategies to address this population. Additionally, schools are becoming more diverse than they have been in the past. This societal change is requiring school psychologists to become more culturally aware and sensitive in the intervention methods they use. As a result, the profession as a whole will experience two events: the first is the lack of diversity among school psychologists and the second is an overall short supply of school psychologists to meet the growing demands of schools today.

Contributing to School Knowledge Base

The school psychologist has a responsibility to contribute to the improvement of the curriculum and student services offered at the school. As such, the psychologist should make efforts to participant in, conduct, and publish psychological research. In doing so, the psychologists must follow the guidelines of the National Association of School Psychologist and their specific school for conducting research with human participants. This will include obtaining permission from a review board to conduct the research as well as obtaining permission from participants (or their parents) to report and present research findings.

Ethical Codes and Conduct

Ethical codes are put in place by committees in order to provide professional guidelines for conducting business. These codes are often imperfect and do not always cover all situations. Specifically, ethical codes may not reflect the current state of the industry, they are often emotionally reactive in nature, and there may be underlying ethical principles in any given situation. On the other hand, ethical conduct involves the practice of understanding and adhering to ethical codes within the scope of the situation and is based on professional expertise. As a school psychologist, it is important in have a firm understanding of established ethical codes as well as sound principles in order to make educated decisions in situations when ethical codes may be vague.

Conflict of Interest

Conflict of interest occurs when a professional is involved in multiple relationships that may intermingle and violate ethical standards. According to the National Association of School Psychologists' code of ethics, school psychologists must take care in their personal lives not to compromise or intermingle with their professional relationships. In other words, the psychologist must avoid multiple types of relationships with the same individuals. For example, if a psychologist is treating a family, it would be a conflict of interest to invite that family to dinner on the weekend and begin developing a personal relationship. Additionally, the psychologist may not exploit a professional relationship and should be careful that personal judgments are not influenced by professional relationships.

Students with Disabilities Legislation

The first assumption is that schools define a discrepancy in the student's ability based on what is expected and what is observed. In other words, if a student is expected to understand their multiplication tables from zero to ten by third grade, a student who is unable to do this may be identified as having a learning disability. The second assumption is that there are students who demonstrate an academic or behavioral discrepancy that cannot be addressed effectively within the general school curriculum. Therefore, it is necessary to modify the general curriculum in order to assist these students in meeting the requirements necessary for academic success and promotion. The final assumption is that it is the responsibility of educators to develop a number of plans, implement these plans, and assess the plans in order to determine the most effective intervention plan for their students.

Educational History

Information that should be collected in terms of educational history will include reviewing previous academic records as well as conducting parent interviews in order to gather information about where the student has been educated, what language the student has been educated in, previous bilingual education services, the number of schools the student has attended, areas of academic success, and failure in the areas of academic concerns. In collecting this history, school psychologists should note if any academic concerns relate to all languages the student speaks.

Language History

This information will include gathering information on the languages that the student knows how to speak as well as languages that are spoken at home, what language the student prefers to speak, what language(s) the student knows how to read, and in what language(s) the student watches television and listens to music.

Drug Classification

Drugs are categorized based on their chemical structure and use. For example, the group of drugs used to treat depression is called antidepressants.

Pharmacotherapeutics is the study of pharmacology geared toward examining the sources and properties of a drug in order to determine how to best use the drug for treatment or the prevention of a disease.

Target symptoms refers to those symptoms that are affected by a specific drug. For example, individuals suffering depression and taking an antidepressant will experience fewer or no depressive symptoms because the drug may enhance chemicals in the brain such as serotonin or dopamine.

ANTIPSYCHOTICS

Antipsychotics are medications intended to treat bizarre behaviors displayed by individuals experiencing psychosis. Today, this class of medications is further categorized into typical and atypical antipsychotics. Bizarre behaviors include hallucinations, delusions, hyperactivity, and abnormal agitation or behavior, and are typically used to treat individuals with the diagnosis of schizophrenia and its subtypes, mania, and major depressive disorders. Antipsychotics work by altering dopamine levels since excess dopamine levels is a primary cause of these symptoms. While these medications are beneficial in treating positive symptoms of these disorders such as hallucinations and delusions, they are not as effective in treating negative symptoms such as cognitive impairments, flat affect, and withdrawal.

Review Video: Antipsychotic Drugs
Visit mometrix.com/academy and enter code: 369601

ANTIDEPRESSANTS

Antidepressants are prescribed to treat major depression, bipolar disorder, anxiety disorders, and other mood disorders. Within the class of antidepressants are subclasses including tricyclic antidepressants, serotonin reuptake inhibitors, and monoamine oxidase inhibitors. This type of medication works on the neurochemical dopamine. The use of antidepressants varies as does its treatment and side effects. For the most part, antidepressants work to reduce the symptoms of various levels of depression and mood disorders. However, side effects range from weight gain to suicidal thoughts. When using antidepressants for treatment, it is important to understand the individual differences that will determine the effectiveness and side effects of these drugs.

MOOD STABILIZERS

Mood stabilizers are most commonly used to treat mania and bipolar disorder, and often include lithium or a variation of this chemical. Mood stabilizers affect various processes in the brain including decreasing certain chemicals or creating biological changes in the brain. Since lithium can be fatal in large doses, medical supervision of this type of treatment is required. Side effects of mood stabilizers vary but may include headaches, fatigue, and weight gain. While the primary treatment purpose of this class of medication is bipolar disorder, other disorders may benefit from these types of drugs including extreme aggression, anorexia nervosa, various phobias, and schizoaffective disorder.

ANXIOLYTICS

Anxiolytics are medications used to treat anxiety and include benzodiazepines, antidepressants, propranolol, and azaspirodecanediones. These drugs are Schedule IV controlled substances because of their potential for substance abuse. Anxiolytics work by relaxing muscles or serving as sedatives and most forms increase the inhibition of y-aminobutyric acid (GABA), a neurotransmitter within the central nervous system. This class of drug may treat some anxiety disorders such as panic disorder, post traumatic stress disorder, and obsessive-compulsive disorder. Since this class of drugs focuses on the central nervous system, many of the side effects experienced are also associated with this system and include weakness, ataxia, dysarthria, and drowsiness.

Hypnotics

Hypnotics are commonly used to treat insomnia, however are only a temporary solution. After prolonged use of hypnotics, the treatment effects wear off and they are no longer effective. These drugs chemically induce sleep; however, many physicians may attempt alternative solutions to an individual's insomnia, such as meditation. Of note, due to their potential to be abused, these drugs are often classified as Schedule II, III, or IV for controlled substances. In addition to insomnia, hypnotics are also used during surgery as an anesthetic; however, the individual does not typically experience a normal restful sleep while on this form of hypnotic.

Drug Use Continuum

The drug use continuum follows four stages. In the first stage, or the experimental stage, the adolescent will typically use a drug to try it out due to peer pressure. During this stage, there is no regular use of a drug and, typically, the user is aware of the dangers of prolonged use. The second stage is social use. During this stage, use of a drug is during social situations, which is slightly more regular than use during the experimental stage and is commonly a result of withdrawal effects experienced in the experimental stage. The third stage, operation use, may also be considered abuse. During this stage, a user may be considered a pleasure-pursuant user or a pain-avoidant user. The final stage of this continuum is dependent use. During this stage, abuse has become addiction and the individual must use the drug in order to avoid withdrawal effects.

Alcohol Abuse

Alcohol is a depressant that affects the central nervous system. For example, alcohol decreases judgment, reaction time, and heart rate. Use and abuse of alcohol can lead to various physiological deficits including issues with the liver, immune system, and brain. Alcohol use among adolescents can cause additional longer term issues, both physically and socially. In addition to the effects of alcohol intake, withdrawal from the substance may include disorientation, seizures, and agitation. Social issues of alcohol abuse include drunken driving and aggression. Also, infants born to alcoholic mothers are often diagnosed with fetal alcohol syndrome. Reports suggest that significant numbers of adolescents who use alcohol also experience psychological and behavioral problems.

Substance Abuse Intervention

Step 1

Early identification. Substance abuse interventions are often more effective when the problem is identified in the beginning stages of use or abuse. Therefore, adults are encouraged to learn and understand the signs of possible substance use, including changes in behavior, grades, appearance, friends, or events such as increases in tardiness for school or truancy.

Step 2

Assessment of the level or stage of the abuse. This is typically conducted by a professional, such as the school's psychologist and involves interviewing the student, teachers, parents, as well as assessing student records.

Step 3

Referral to the appropriate social services or school or community program.

Step 4

Follow up. Assess the student to monitor the intervention and determine its effectiveness.

Adaptive Roles Children of Substance Abusers Take On

In many homes where one or both parents are substance abusers, members of the family will fall into one of five main roles.

1. Chief-enabler. This individual will often make excuses for the user as well as provide support for the user to continue. The chief enabler often receives special attention from the user because he is on the user's side.
2. Family hero. This individual is the perfectionist of the family. The family hero typically does well in school and provides a good public front for the family.
3. Scapegoat. This individual is typically the trouble maker of the family and is often blamed for the family's problems.
4. Lost child. This individual often keeps to himself as a means to deal with the family situation.
5. Mascot. Typically, the "funny one" this individuals handles stress by being the class clown.

School-Based Substance Abuse Prevention Program

School-based prevention programs benefit the entire school. These programs are most beneficial when they are consistent from kindergarten through twelfth grade and provide regular information and support to the students. These programs should also offer students with an organized and regular curriculum of information, employing various education methods, including group work, feedback, and reinforcement. Additionally, a school-based prevention program should focus on and support prosocial behaviors within the school and community. Finally, these programs should be scientifically evaluated annually to determine their effectiveness as well as determine any necessary changes for improvement.

Working with a Child of a Substance Abuser

Working with children of substance abusers poses unique challenges. Family conflict is often prevalent in these homes and may include violence. In this environment, the child may have difficulty sleeping or getting homework completed, thus affecting their academics. Inconsistent discipline or structure in the home is another factor affecting these children. These children may experience overly strict discipline at times and no discipline other times. Additionally, these children may have little or no supervision or support at home. Role reversal also occurs when the child is placed in the role of the parent. Rather than the child being able to be a child, he is required or feels obligated to care for his using parent or for other siblings in the house.

When working with a child of a substance abuser, consistency and support are essential elements to consider. There are four main guidelines for these situations.

1. Develop and maintain a daily schedule for the child. This will offer the child structure and order, at least while at school.
2. Enable the child by allowing them to make their own choices. This practice will help the child learn effective problem solving and decision making techniques as well as increase self-confidence.
3. Include additional time for the child to complete homework while still at school.
4. Monitor the child regularly in order to identify stress or tension, and deal with these emotions immediately.

ABC crisis intervention model

(A) Developing and maintaining contact

The first step in any therapeutic relationship is developing a positive working relationship. Due to the nature of this relationship, it is important that the student trusts the therapist. This relationship begins during the initial interview and is effective when the therapist presents himself or herself as empathetic and nonjudgmental.

(B) Identifying the problem and therapeutic interaction

It is often necessary to identify the problem quickly. Therefore, focusing on the crisis or situation affecting the child is essential to success.

(C) Coping

During this phase, the therapist and the client work together to identify new ways of seeing and handling a situation. The therapist may offer information about stress reduction techniques or problem solving strategies.

Systems and psychoanalytic theory

Systems theory

Systems theory studies the family in crisis situations. Following this theory the psychologist believes that the family, as a system, is self sustaining and can correct itself when the system becomes broken. In other words, when one family member steps out of his role, the other family members will compensate in order to maintain family order.

Psychoanalytic theory

Psychoanalytic theory focuses on the life of the individual rather than simply one crisis at a time. However, in crisis situations, the psychologist following psychoanalytic theory will examine all factors of the individual's life in order to treat the specific crisis. The focus here is typically on the ego, superego, and the id.

National Institute on Drug Abuse guidelines

Substance abuse programs that involve the family are beneficial because they garner support from the community and the parents in preventing substance abuse. The National Institute on Drug Abuse suggests the following guidelines when developing such a program. First, educating parents on various matters including positive reinforcement, communication, problem solving, rulemaking, and monitoring activities is important. These skills provide parents with the means to effectively communicate with and support their children. Second, parents learn the various developmental stages of childhood, which allows the parents to be aware of what to expect as their child grows as well as how to approach the child at different ages. Finally, these programs educate parents on drug related information and offer counseling and other support systems for the family to utilize if necessary.

Ineffective substance abuse programs

There are many substance prevention programs that have been proven unworthy and ineffective over the years. Among these include information-only programs, scare tactics, one-shot programs, and values-clarification programs. Information-only programs are beneficial for providing basic information about the physical and legal effects of drug use; however, these programs have never been shown to alleviate use or abuse when presented alone. Scare tactics attempt to show adolescents the effects of substance use gone wrong; however, they do little to offer support in avoiding use in the first place. One-shot programs that may include one film or one assembly during the school year are also ineffective because they do not provide all the necessary information and there is no follow up. Finally, values-clarification programs serve only to enforce old or current values and do not offer support of the development of new values. These programs are especially ineffective if the individual's values do not include concern for substance abuse.

Practice Test

Want to take this practice test in an online interactive format?
Check out the online resources page, which includes interactive practice questions and much more: **mometrix.com/resources719/clepintedpsy**

1. Which of these is correct about characteristics of the interview process?

a. Establishing a relationship with the respondent will only interfere
b. Most often the interview questions are standardized for uniformity
c. Good interviewers focus only on information, not on social factors
d. Rapport will create the trust needed to share personal information
e. Interviews are the same as questionnaires, but spoken, not written

2. What is true about observational measures used by psychologists?

a. Observations focus only on the processes of behavior
b. Observations focus only on the products of behavior
c. Observations conducted must be by direct observation
d. Observations must be only via naturalistic observation
e. Observations can be all of these; no one answer is sufficient

3. At the beginning of the school year, for a new student with no previous assessments or school records which of these would be least indicated for problem identification?

a. Complete IQ testing
b. Portfolio assessments
c. Personality inventory
d. Tests for social skills
e. Speech/hearing tests

4. The Activity-Based Assessment Inventory, or ABA Inventory, is not designed to explore which area of a student's life?

a. Family
b. Friends
c. Grades
d. Games
e. Groups

5. What is true regarding the Child Behavior Checklist (CBCL)?

a. The information it collects is reported by a child's parents
b. It assesses behavior problems but not social competencies
c. It is a self-report measure, so interviewers are not allowed
d. Its items are not standardized and they can be individualized
e. It is designed for pre-school and elementary school students

6. For which teachers would the History/Transition Information Profile be most useful?

a. "Step-up" teachers who follow their students from one grade to the next
b. Teachers of mixed-age classes with the same students for several years
c. Teachers with a class of all new students who have past school records
d. Teachers with a class of all new students with no earlier school records
e. Teachers of all these kinds of classes could benefit equally from its use

7. Which of the following people developed the first working intelligence test?

a. Alfred Binet
b. Lewis Terman
c. David Wechsler
d. Raymond Cattell
e. Howard Gardner

8. Of the following tests, which is not a standardized achievement test?

a. The ITBS
b. The CTBS
c. The SAT
d. The CAT
e. The TAT

9. In the Wechsler Intelligence Scale for Children (WISC), which of the following subtests evaluates short-term memory?

a. Vocabulary
b. Digit Span
c. Block Design
d. Symbol Search
e. Picture Concepts

10. What is not a type of executive function that students must use to succeed in school?

a. Being able to retrieve previously learned information
b. Being able to organize a report, essay, or project parts
c. Being able to assign appropriate priority to each item
d. Being able to follow specific, step-by-step directions
e. Being able to manage work time in a realistic fashion

11. Research finds that which of these is most effective for developing phonemic awareness?

a. Oral language teaching only
b. Print language teaching only
c. Both oral and print teaching
d. None of these is found most effective
e. Any of these is equally as good as any other

12. Which of the following tests is not designed for assessing children's social skills?

a. SSRS
b. SIB-R
c. Vineland
d. Peabody
e. Walker-McConnell

13. What is the most accurate statement relative to assessment of students?

a. It is important to assess both intellectual ability and adaptive behavior
b. It is more important to assess adaptive behavior than intellectual ability
c. It is more important to assess intellectual ability than adaptive behavior
d. Either may be assessed, but both are not needed as they usually match
e. Neither adaptive behavior nor intellectual ability is important to assess

14. A typical elementary school student is most often in which of Erikson's psychosocial stages of development?

a. Trust vs. Mistrust
b. Autonomy vs. Shame and Doubt
c. Initiative vs. Guilt
d. Industry vs. Inferiority
e. Identity vs. Role Confusion

15. For conducting a functional behavior assessment, which of these should be done first?

a. Collect information on possible functions of the behavior
b. Collect information to assess and describe the behavior
c. Collect information to refine definition of the behavior
d. Collect information to verify how serious the behavior is
e. It does not matter in which order these steps are executed

16. Of the following personality theorists, who did not propose a personality type theory?

a. Hippocrates
b. Galen
c. William Sheldon
d. Frank Sulloway
e. Gordon Allport

17. Which of these is not one of McCrae and Costa's "Big Five" personality traits?

a. Neuroticism
b. Psychoticism
c. Agreeableness
d. Conscientiousness
e. Openness to experience

18. What is the correct chronological order of Freud's five stages of psychosexual development?

a. Latency, Oral, Anal, Phallic, Genital
b. Phallic, Oral, Anal, Genital, Latency
c. Oral, Anal, Phallic, Latency, Genital
d. Anal, Oral, Genital, Phallic, Latency
e. Genital, Latency, Phallic, Oral, Anal

19. According to some researchers (Herman et al 1992, O'Malley & Valdez Pierce, 1996), all performance-based assessments have certain characteristics. Which of these is not included in performance-based assessment?

a. Norm-referenced tests
b. Process plus product
c. An integrative quality
d. Authenticity of design
e. Depth and not breadth

20. Which of the following is not an advantage of curriculum-based assessment?

a. The scoring is objective
b. Validity and reliability
c. Practical to administer
d. Detects small changes
e. No need to give often

21. According to Piaget's theory of cognitive development, when assessing a developmentally normal four-year-old, which of these tasks would be most appropriate?

a. Liquid conservation
b. Object permanence
c. Pretend play games
d. Oral logic questions
e. Any of these would be equally appropriate

22. According to the Standards for Educational and Psychological Testing (AERA, APA, & NCME, 1999), what is not one of the most important criteria for high technical quality of assessments?

a. Validity
b. Reliability
c. Lack of bias
d. All of these
e. None of these

23. Which of the following is not one of the categories of evidence that can be used to verify test validity?

a. How much the content of the assessment aligns with standards
b. How much consistency exists among different raters of the test
c. How the assessment is related to other measures of proficiency
d. How much accurate results are ensured in the response process
e. How much statistically proven reliability, validity, balance exist

24. Test reliability is compromised by error in an assessment instrument. Which of these is not a main source of error in testing?

a. Factors in the test that is given
b. Factors in students being tested
c. Factors in the scoring of the test
d. These are all main error sources
e. None of these is a source of error

25. Test results can be less accurate and/or less valid when bias is present. Two common sources of bias are race or ethnicity and cultural differences. Which of these is not another source of bias in testing?

a. Gender
b. Disability
c. Language
d. Geography
e. They all are

26. Which of these is not a meaning included in the term ipsative (assessment, measurement, or scoring)?

a. These are all meanings included among definitions of the term "ipsative"
b. Comparing a student's current score to the same student's previous score
c. Comparing scoring of different subtests within the same test instrument
d. Comparing a student's scores on different scales, equating score variance
e. Assessment by means of forced choices as opposed to Likert-type scales

27. Joseph Renzulli (2005) has proposed that IQ score alone is insufficient to define giftedness. In his "three-ring conception of giftedness," all except which of the following is included?

a. Ability
b. Creativity
c. Versatility
d. Task commitment
e. None of these

28. Using standardized IQ tests, these students had the following results: Johnny's score was below 20. Jill's score was 102. Jackie's score was 67. Albert's score was 123. Gail's score was 154. Based on these scores, which of these statements is not correct?

a. Johnny has profound intellectual disability
b. Jackie has moderate intellectual disability
c. Jill's intelligence is considered average
d. Albert's IQ is considered above average
e. Gail's score is considered highly gifted

29. Which of these is not a measure of central tendency in statistics?

a. Range
b. Mean
c. Mode
d. Median
e. All are

30. What is not an accurate statement regarding correlations?

a. A correlation coefficient of 0 means there is no consistent relationship between two variables
b. A strong negative correlation means if scores are high on one variable, they are low on the other
c. A strong positive correlation means if scores are high on one variable, they are high on the other
d. A correlation coefficient of +1 is a perfect positive correlation; -1 is a perfect negative correlation
e. A perfect positive correlation between two variables means that one will always cause the other

31. Which of the following is not a characteristic of descriptive statistics?

a. Measures of central tendency
b. Statistical significance
c. Measures of variability
d. Correlation coefficients
e. Frequency distributions

32. In experimental research, which of the following is manipulated by the researcher(s)?

a. An independent variable
b. A dependent variable
c. A confounding variable
d. None of these variables
e. All of these variables

33. If you had identified a group of children placed in an early intervention program as preschoolers and you wanted to see whether the salutary effects of the program, as measured at the end of the year, were maintained in these children five years later, what type of research design would you be most likely to use?

a. Cross-sectional design
b. Cross-sequential design
c. Longitudinal design
d. Any of these designs
e. None of these designs

34. Steele (1973) identified six types or categories of approaches in program evaluation. Two are evaluation as input into decision-making and evaluation processes models. Which of the following is not one of the other four?

a. Kinds of data and activities
b. Evaluation of program parts
c. Results: objectives attainment
d. Results: outcomes and effects
e. These are all identified types

35. What is not true about quantitative and qualitative research methods when used in program evaluation?

a. Quantitative methods make it easier to generalize the research findings
b. Quantitative methods make it easier to summarize and compare groups
c. Qualitative methods make it easier to go into greater depth and detail
d. Quantitative methods and qualitative methods are mutually exclusive
e. Quantitative validity depends on instruments, qualitative on researchers

36. Learning certain social skills is a requisite to the success of cooperative learning groups. One of these is leadership. Which of the following is not one of others?

a. Decision-making
b. Problem-solving
c. Trust-building
d. Communication
e. Conflict management

37. According to researchers in educational psychology, cooperative learning requires five conditions to be productive. One condition is that social skills are taught (#36 above). Which of the following is not one of the other four conditions?

a. Positive interdependence in the group
b. Face-to-face interaction in the group
c. Individual and group accountability
d. Group processing among members
e. Fostering competition of members

38. Which is most correct about Vygotsky's concept of scaffolding?

a. It is given as needed and gradually withdrawn as competency grows
b. It is support given to children in advance of their learning new things
c. It is a structure built to support children who cannot stand up or walk
d. It is a type of assistance provided to learners throughout their lifespan
e. It is provided for a specified limited time and then abruptly removed

39. What is an example of Vygotsky's zone of proximal development?

a. An adult teacher assigns children exercises just beyond their ability
b. Two or three children on the same academic level help one another
c. A child who is slightly more advanced helps another child to learn
d. Children using various approaches to a task combine their findings
e. A child developing a new skill moves to the next level of difficulty

40. The Individuals with Disabilities Education Act (IDEA) mandates that if assistive technology (AT) devices or services are needed for a student with disabilities to access a free and appropriate public education (FAPE), they must be provided. The Office of Special Education and Rehabilitative Services (OSERS) has clarified the law on a number of points. Which of the following does not correctly describe one of these points?

a. AT must be supplied to the student's family at no cost by the school district
b. AT's necessity to assure a FAPE must be determined on a case-by-case basis
c. The student's IEP must show the kind of AT and extent of support services
d. If the student's IEP specifies AT is needed, it is for school but not home use
e. Parents are given comprehensive procedural safeguards including giving AT

41. Three students are starting the same new class at the beginning of the school year. On the first day before class, Pat says, "I want to get the highest grade of anybody in this class." Chris says, "I just don't want to flunk out of this class." Mia says, "I want to learn all there is to know about this class." Which of the following statements is not correct about these students?

a. Pat and Mia have performance-approach goals
b. Chris evidences a performance-avoidance goal
c. Pat demonstrates a performance-approach goal
d. Mia's goal orientation is that of a mastery goal
e. None of these statements is correct about goals

42. Classmates are discussing their scores on a recent test. Courtney says, "I'm glad I studied so hard for this test; that's why I got such a high grade." Britney says, "I got a high grade too, but I didn't study hard; I was just lucky." Bert says, "It's my own fault I got a low grade; I stayed up too late playing games with my friends and didn't review before the test." Ernie says, "My grade stinks! It's not fair; the teacher hates me and I can't win." According to Julian Rotter (1966), which statement is accurate regarding locus of control in these students?

a. Courtney demonstrates external locus of control
b. Britney demonstrates an internal locus of control
c. Courtney and Bert have internal loci of control
d. Courtney and Ernie have external loci of control
e. Britney and Ernie display internal loci of control

43. In studying achievement motivation, David McClelland has labeled the need for achievement as n Ach. Which of the following is not true about some of his findings?

a. Sons with high n Ach scores tended to surpass their fathers' job status
b. Individuals with high n Ach scores will work harder to achieve goals
c. Individuals with high n Ach scores will give up difficult tasks earlier
d. Individuals with high n Ach scores require more efficiency/less effort
e. Individuals with high n Ach scores had more early parental pressures

44. In a 1975 longitudinal study of over 26,000 children (Broman et al), which factor(s) was/were found most predictive of a child's IQ score at age 4?

a. The IQ test scores of both of the child's parents
b. The IQ test score of the child's mother only
c. The educational level of the child's mother
d. Socioeconomic status and mother's education
e. Socioeconomic status and parents' education

45. Manuel's parents are Latino immigrants to the United States. Manuel was born in the US and enters school speaking fluent English. His teacher gives him a negative evaluation because he never volunteers to answer questions or speaks up in class. What is the most likely explanation for this based on the information given?

a. Manuel is uncomfortable with speaking English
b. The teacher is prejudiced against Latino students
c. Manuel is shy and afraid to answer incorrectly
d. Manuel is not as intelligent as the other students
e. Manuel has different cultural values about school

46. The High School and Beyond survey (Gamoran & Mare, 1989) studied the effects of academic tracking in high school. Which of these is not true about the study's findings?

a. Placement in the college track improved achievement in mathematics
b. Placement in the college track raised chances of high school graduation
c. Tracking reduced achievement differences in students of different SES
d. Tracking reduced the differences in achievement between boys and girls
e. Tracking reduced differences in achievement between blacks and whites

47. Which of the following is not true about English Language Learners (ELLs) in American schools?

a. From 1986-2006 ELL population grew 14 times more than general school population
b. The ELL population in America as a group speaks more than 400 different languages
c. Projections are that by 2015, 30% of school-age children in the USA will be ELLs
d. Of the ELL population in America, 50 percent speak Spanish as their first language
e. The most ELLs are 1st-generation Americans and those who arrived before age five

48. In providing Positive Behavioral Support in the classroom, which of these is not a preventive strategy for the physical classroom environment?

a. Keeping areas with high traffic free of congestion
b. Keeping furniture setups constant once arranged
c. Being sure the teacher can easily see the students
d. Keeping often-used materials and supplies handy
e. Being sure students can see presentations easily

49. Positive behavioral support in the classroom dictates that the teacher's communication of expectations to students should have all but which of these qualities?

a. They should be as thorough and detailed as possible
b. They should be few in number, such as three to five
c. They should be stated in positive, not negative terms
d. They should be concisely stated in simple sentences
e. They should be enforceable, i.e. observable behaviors

50. Dan Olweus' famous Bullying Prevention Program has components at four levels. Which of the following is not one of these levels?

a. School-level components
b. Individual-level components
c. Classroom-level components
d. Community-level components
e. School system-level components

51. Of the following, which educational level was the Olweus Bullying Prevention Program not specifically researched and designed for, but has also used the program for bullying?

a. Elementary school
b. Middle school
c. Junior high school
d. High school
e. None of these

52. In recent years, school safety has become an increasingly important issue. Educators point to which of the following as factors contributing to the need for school safety?

a. More students from dysfunctional families
b. More students from impoverished families
c. More students with parents who are teens
d. More students requiring special education
e. More students from all of these categories

53. In implementing a safe-school plan, which of these would not be a goal for school administrators?

a. Providing leadership in developing, monitoring, and evaluating the plan
b. Setting up a program of constant tracking and reporting of school crime
c. Being models of pro-social behavior as well as teaching school subjects
d. Assuring safe traffic to, from, and within schools by environment design
e. Establishing procedures for crisis management and emergency evacuation

54. A school safety council should include all except which of these as representatives?

a. Members of the school's staff
b. Students attending the school
c. Some of the students' parents
d. Members from the community
e. All of these should be included

55. Which of the following is not correct regarding applied behavior analysis (ABA)?

a. ABA is not known to be as effective in classroom learning as it is with autism
b. ABA is often the preferred treatment for behavior problems related to intellectual disability
c. ABA has produced very significant results with autism spectrum disorders
d. ABA has been quite successful in working with people with brain injuries
e. All of these statements are correct with regard to applied behavior analysis

56. Of the following, which is not an appropriate activity for a school counselor?

a. Helping individual students plan their academic programs
b. Conducting clinical therapy 1:1 with individual students
c. Group counseling with small and large groups of students
d. Counseling students who have problems with discipline
e. Attending students' IEP meetings to advocate for them

57. With regard to developmentally appropriate practices, what is not true about early childhood education and special education?

a. Both fields stress the importance of individualized intervention and programs
b. Assessment of children's progress must be multidimensional and naturalistic
c. Learning must be personally relevant for children with and without disabilities
d. Federal law dictates that each of these fields has separate, exclusive programs
e. All these statements are true regarding early childhood and special education

58. Those teaching conflict resolution to children advocate four things they need to do. Which of the following is not one of these things?

a. Understand
b. Don't make things worse
c. Take charge
d. Work together
e. Find the solution

59. According to the Crisis Management Institute's training for crisis management planning, which is not a level at which crisis planning takes place?

a. Building
b. Classroom
c. District
d. Team
e. Community

60. Which of these instruments would not be used to assess school climate?

a. All of these would be used as school climate assessment instruments
b. Education, Training, Research Character Education Survey (2000)
c. Tribes Assessment Questionnaire (1996)
d. CASE-1987
e. SCCP-2000

61. Of the following diagnoses that a student might have, which would not be found in the DSM-5?

a. Cystic fibrosis
b. Schizophrenia with childhood onset
c. Antisocial personality disorder
d. Speech Sound Disorder
e. These would all be found in the DSM-5

62. With the DSM-5 incorporating so many changes in its structure, Jack feels confused about how to use it for assigning diagnoses required for treatment plans. What is the MOST effective way for him to gain expertise in the new DSM?

a. Ask colleagues for advice on his paperwork.
b. Read the DSM-5 cover to cover.
c. Attend a professional seminar on using the updated DSM in practice.
d. Put off his paperwork until he is more comfortable with the new format.
e. Continue to use the old DSM instead.

63. What change in the DSM-5 better aligns it with global healthcare organizations?

a. It refined the Global Assessment of Functioning (GAF).
b. It added the World Health Organization's Disability Assessment Schedule to Section III.
c. It replaced Axis IV with psychosocial context.
d. It eliminated the GAF.
e. It ceased using the axis system to classify disorders.

64. Which of the following is least likely to be a sign of substance abuse in a student?

a. The student's grades suddenly fall dramatically
b. The student tells you all about personal problems
c. The student is uncharacteristically truant/absent
d. The student has lost interest in favorite subjects
e. The student's attention span and memory are reduced

65. For which of these would it not be appropriate for the school to request a behavioral consultation?

a. A student diagnosed with autism spectrum disorder
b. A student who has a diagnosis of a bipolar disorder
c. Any of these if behavior problems are serious enough
d. Students with attention deficit/hyperactivity disorder
e. Students who are identified as emotionally disturbed

66. In the best early childhood programs, what is not true about the roles of mental health consultants?

a. Mental health consultants in early childhood programs do not as a rule conduct direct therapeutic interventions with the children enrolled in the programs
b. Mental health consultants in early childhood programs inform, teach, and support teachers and administrators on behavior and developmental delays
c. Mental health consultants in early childhood programs consult with teachers or teams to resolve problems with an individual child and/or child's family
d. Mental health consultants in early childhood programs may coach parents to interact more effectively with their children when they are in their home
e. Mental health consultants in early childhood programs can help families access and use diagnostic and therapeutic MH services outside the program

67. According to the University of Maryland's laboratory for instructional consultation teams, which of these is the goal of IC teams as opposed to an objective of IC teams?

a. To establish a support network, with a trained IC team, in every building
b. To improve teacher skills and use of best practices in testing and teaching
c. To develop norms school-wide for working together and solving problems
d. To enhance, improve, and increase the performance of students and staff
e. To make use of available data for making decisions in the class and school

68. According to the Indiana School Boards Association, which of these statements is not correct regarding school board policy?

a. School board policies should determine a definite course of action for schools
b. School board policies should tell administrators what they are supposed to do
c. School board policies should tell administrators how to do what they should do
d. School board policies, in some cases, have been determined by certain legislation
e. School board policies, in some cases, are determined according to common sense

69. Which of these brain structures is most associated with the formation of explicit memory?

a. The hypothalamus
b. The hippocampus
c. The cerebellum
d. The amygdala
e. The thalamus

70. A student returns to school following a head injury. You find that this student now displays new problems with making up her mind, planning her activities, and setting goals for herself. Which lobe of the student's brain is most likely to be damaged?

a. Frontal
b. Parietal
c. Temporal
d. Occipital
e. All four

71. Which of the following is not true about findings of research into schizophrenia?

a. The risk of schizophrenia for children whose parents both have it is 46 times greater than in the general population
b. The probability for identical twins both having schizophrenia is about three times higher than for fraternal twins
c. Neither emotional reactivity nor environmental stressors were found to affect schizophrenia symptoms
d. Brain imaging has shown that many people with schizophrenia have larger brain ventricles than normal brains
e. Brain scans have shown that brains of adolescents with schizophrenia lost a great deal more gray matter over 5 years

72. Research into schizophrenia has found that which of the following environmental factors is/are associated with higher rates of the illness?

a. Living in urban environments
b. Having economic difficulties
c. Migration to another country
d. Traumatic events in one's life
e. Research identifies all of these

73. You are told that a student suffers from Wernicke's aphasia. You would expect this student to:

a. Have difficulty understanding what you say
b. Have difficulty expressing himself verbally
c. Have difficulty hearing things that you say
d. Have difficulty with spelling and grammar
e. Have difficulty with all of these processes

74 Which of these is not a common characteristic of autism spectrum disorders?

a. Repetitive and ritualistic behaviors
b. Difficulty with social interactions
c. Not understanding others' feelings
d. Having a very short attention span
e. Difficulty with changes in routines

75. With reference to Pavlov's classical conditioning experiments, which of the following is correct?

a. The food was a conditioned stimulus
b. The food was an unconditioned stimulus
c. The tone was an unconditioned stimulus
d. Salivation was always an unconditioned response
e. Salivation was always a conditioned response

76. What is not true about classical conditioning and operant conditioning?

a. Classical conditioning was developed earlier in time than operant conditioning
b. Operant conditioning involves voluntary behaviors; classical, involuntary ones
c. Classically conditioned and operant responses are elicited by particular stimuli
d. Operant conditioning can change a behavior by manipulating its consequences
e. All of these choices are true of classical conditioning and operant conditioning

77. Who of the following researchers has/have viewed adolescence as a period of great turbulence?

a. G. Stanley Hall
b. Margaret Mead
c. Ruth Benedict
d. Jeffrey Arnett
e. All of these

78. Charlie's teacher yells at him in school. He goes home and yells at his little sister. Which of Freud's ego defense mechanisms does this illustrate?

a. Projection
b. Displacement
c. Regression
d. Sublimation
e. Reaction formation

79. Whose personality theory is not a cognitive theory?

a. Albert Bandura
b. Walter Mischel
c. Nancy Cantor
d. Julian Rotter
e. Carl Rogers

80. Social psychologist C. Daniel Batson (1994) has proposed four motivations for pro-social behavior, such as the behavior of people (not government agencies) who went out of their way to help victims of such natural disasters as 2005's Hurricane Katrina in the United States, the 2008 earthquake in Sichuan, China, and the 2010 earthquake in Haiti. Which of the following is not one of the motives defined by Batson?

a. Altruism
b. Egoism
c. Collectivism
d. Socialism
e. Principlism

81. Different theorists of intelligence have proposed one or more factors of intelligence. Which pair defined, respectively, the most reductionist and the most expansionist views of intelligence?

a. Spearman; Gardner
b. Cattell; Sternberg
c. Gardner; Sternberg
d. Spearman; Cattell
e. None of these did

82. Of the following theorists of language development, who is not known for subscribing to the idea of linguistic relativity?

a. Edward Sapir
b. Benjamin Whorf
c. Roger Brown
d. Noam Chomsky
e. All of these are

83. Which of these is a limitation of self-reporting measures in testing?

a. Speech and language deficits
b. Some psychological disorders
c. The issue of reporting validity
d. The issue of testing reliability
e. These all represent limitations

84. Who of the following pioneers in the field of psychology was known for making extensive use of naturalistic observation in doing research?

a. Sigmund Freud
b. B. F. Skinner
c. Jean Piaget
d. All of these
e. None of these

85. You are told that a new student in your school has Broca's aphasia. You would expect this student to:

a. Have trouble understanding what you say
b. Have trouble expressing herself in words
c. Have trouble understanding what she sees
d. Have trouble with her motor coordination
e. Have trouble with none of these functions

86. Which kind of test validity relates to how thoroughly a test measures the complete range of the domain being tested?

a. Content validity
b. Criterion validity
c. Predictive validity
d. Construct validity
e. None of these

87. In formal assessment, split-half reliability:

a. Is measured using parallel test forms
b. Is an indicator of test-retest reliability
c. Is one measure of internal consistency
d. Is described accurately by all of these
e. Is described correctly by none of these

88. In the 1970s, researchers examined items on an IQ test after Black children with lower socioeconomic status got lower scores than White children with higher socioeconomic status. On an item about the logical relationships of objects, the question stem asked what the word "cup" went with, and the choices were "saucer" (the correct choice), "table," "fork," or "chair." While most higher-SES White children chose "saucer," many lower-SES Black children chose "table." The researchers concluded that this was due to:

a. Cognitive impairment caused by poverty
b. A lack of proper vocabulary development
c. An inherent racial disparity in intelligence
d. An unfair cultural bias in the testing items
e. All of these factors plus their interactions

89. The Principles for Professional Ethics of the NASP's Professional Conduct Manual for School Psychology lists six general principles under the General heading of the Professional Competency section. One of these is that school psychologists know and apply the Principles in their practices. Which of the following is not one of the others?

a. Recognizing the strengths and limitations of their training and experience
b. Not informing their clients of the details of their education and experience
c. Not using their affiliations to mislead clients about their competence levels
d. Pursuing continuing professional development to stay current in their field
e. Not letting personal problems or conflicts compromise their professionalism

90. The American Psychological Association (APA)'s ethical principles give guidelines for the use of intentional deception in research, as in some studies it would bias the results to inform participants of everything in advance. One guideline is that participants should not be misled as to the probability of physical or emotional distress the study could cause. Which of the following are additional APA guidelines regarding deception?

a. The research must be important enough to science and education to justify deception
b. Researchers must show that no procedures just as effective, using no deception, exist
c. Participants must have the deception explained to them after the study has concluded
d. Participants must have the option to remove their data once the deception is revealed
e. All of these statements represent additional APA guidelines with regard to deception

91. Stanley Milgram's (1965) classic experiments on obedience to authority were very valuable to psychologists' understanding of human behavior, but they could not be replicated today because they would violate ethical principles. Which of the following is not true about these experiments?

a. The participants did not go through the current informed consent process
b. The procedures used would violate current APA guidelines on deception
c. The procedures used would not withstand today's risk/gain assessments
d. The participants were not provided a debriefing following the procedure
e. All of these statements are true about Milgram's obedience experiments

92. The Principles for Professional Ethics of the NASP's Professional Conduct Manual for School Psychology lists four general principles involving Students under the Professional Relationships section. Which of the following does not correctly state one of these principles?

a. School psychologists' professional practices should maintain children's dignity
b. They should explain aspects of these relationships clearly and age-appropriately
c. They should not discuss recommendations for program changes or more services
d. They respect a child's right to voluntarily initiate, participate in, or end services
e. All of these correctly state the general principles about professional relationships

93. The Principles for Professional Ethics of the NASP's Professional Conduct Manual for School Psychology lists seven general principles for the Use of Materials and Technology under the Professional Practices section. One of these is that they maintain test security for each instrument used. Another is that they not accept any compensation in return for sharing data from their client database without first obtaining informed consent. Which of the following does not correctly state one of the other five principles?

a. They get prior written consent or remove identifying data for public presentations
b. Software publishers are responsible for ethical/legal use of all technology services
c. They do not use computerized test scoring systems in which they have no training
d. All applications of technology that will lower the quality of service are eschewed
e. Student/client records are not electronically transferred without a privacy guarantee

94. The NASP's Professional Conduct Manual for School Psychology contains Guidelines for the Provision of School Psychological Services. The first of its Practice Guidelines state that school psychologists collaborate with other team members in using a decision-making process. Which of the following is not listed in the guideline as one of the purposes of this process?

a. To identify academic problems and behavior problems
b. To collect and analyze data to understand the problems
c. To make decisions relative to the delivery of services
d. To evaluate the outcomes of the delivery of services
e. To change services based on evaluation of outcomes

95. Which of the following does not correctly state one of the principles under Practice Guideline 2 of the NASP Professional Conduct Manual for School Psychology's Guidelines for the Provision of School Psychological Services?

a. School psychologists function to maintain the status quo at all levels of the system
b. School psychologists promote healthy learning environments by reducing conflicts
c. School psychologists must transmit information to a large variety of communities
d. School psychologists understand and participate in policy determination processes
e. School psychologists are proficient in systems consultation and making decisions

96. Practice Guideline 5 of the NASP Professional Conduct Manual for School Psychology's Guidelines for the Provision of School Psychological Services includes all but which of the following principles with respect to diversity?

a. School psychologists develop individualized academic and behavioral interventions
b. They recognize and work to end subtle biases in themselves, others, and instruments
c. They further practices that will enable all children to feel welcomed and appreciated
d. Interventions are informed by an appreciation of cultural and individual differences
e. Practice Guideline 5 includes all of these principles with respect to student diversity

97. Which of these does informed consent in experimental research not include?

a. Procedures to be used, risks and benefits
b. Commitment to complete the experiment
c. Privacy and confidentiality of all records
d. Voluntarily discontinuing participation
e. Access to officials for filing grievances

98. What is not true about the history of school psychology?

a. School psychology's origins are concurrent with the origins of psychology
b. School psychology is connected to both clinical and functional psychology
c. School psychology uses educational, but not clinical, psychology principles
d. School psychology began as part of social reforms in the 19th-20th centuries
e. School psychology was a result of compulsory and special education needs

99. Who is considered the father of school psychology?

a. James McKeen Cattell
b. Wilhelm Wundt
c. Arnold Gesell
d. Lightner Witmer
e. G. Stanley Hall

100. What is not true about HIPAA?

a. HIPAA's administration is determined via individual states' laws
b. HIPAA regulates the transmission of student and/or client records
c. HIPAA regulates electronic transmittal of insurance claim records
d. HIPAA dictates standards for protecting privacy of information
e. HIPAA protects health insurance in the event of job change/loss

Answers and Explanations

Question	Answer	Question	Answer	Question	Answer	Question	Answer
1	d	26	a	51	d	76	c
2	e	27	c	52	e	77	a
3	b	28	b	53	c	78	b
4	c	29	a	54	e	79	e
5	a	30	e	55	a	80	d
6	c	31	b	56	b	81	a
7	a	32	a	57	d	82	d
8	e	33	c	58	c	83	e
9	b	34	e	59	b	84	c
10	d	35	d	60	a	85	b
11	c	36	b	61	e	86	a
12	d	37	e	62	d	87	c
13	a	38	a	63	e	88	d
14	d	39	c	64	b	89	b
15	b	40	d	65	c	90	e
16	e	41	a	66	a	91	d
17	b	42	c	67	d	92	c
18	c	43	b	68	c	93	b
19	a	44	d	69	b	94	e
20	e	45	e	70	a	95	a
21	c	46	c	71	c	96	e
22	d	47	d	72	e	97	b
23	b	48	b	73	a	98	c
24	d	49	a	74	d	99	d
25	e	50	e	75	b	100	a

1. D: Establishing a good rapport is key to creating the trust required for the respondent to share personal information with the interviewer. Establishing a relationship with the respondent will not interfere with the interview process (a). Interview questions are not most often standardized for uniformity (b). Standardization is a characteristic of survey questionnaires, but interviews are interactive dialogues. The interviewer pursues additional information by further questioning the respondent. Good interviewers do not concentrate only on information and not on social factors (c). A good interviewer will give equal attention to the social interaction with the respondent, as this can yield equally important insights. Interviews are not standardized like questionnaires but are interactive dialogues; surveys can be self-reports or may have fixed alternative answers (such as yes/no/not sure) whereas psychological interviews will not. Therefore, interviews are not simply oral versions of written questionnaires (e).

2. E: No one answer is true. Psychological observations may focus either on the processes of behavior (a), i.e. what things the subject does and how she/he does them; or on the products of the behavior (b), i.e. the results it produces. Thus observations are not restricted to only one of these in every case. Observations of subjects may be made directly, but this is not always required (c). If the behavior is overt and easy to record, direct observation is appropriate. However, if the psychologist wants to observe behaviors that occur naturally without the subject's knowledge to avoid influencing the behavior, naturalistic observation should be used, but this method is not always required (d).

3. B: Portfolio assessments would be least indicated. Portfolio assessments are performance-based and contain products of the student's learning. At the beginning of the school year a new student with no previous assessments or school records will not have a portfolio. A portfolio assessment reflects a student's progress over the school year in a given area. For problem identification with a new student who has no records, a school psychologist would administer such instruments as comprehensive IQ testing scales (a) to determine intellectual levels; personality inventories (c) to learn about the student's individual psychological makeup; tests to determine the student's social skills (d) including strengths and weaknesses; and tests of hearing and speech (e) to identify or rule out hearing deficits and speech problems, as well as tests of language development.

4. C: ABA Inventory is not designed to explore a student's grades. It is designed to explore a student's activities outside of class. It covers the student's role as a member of his or her family (a); the student's role as a friend (b) with others; the kinds of games (d), hobbies, or crafts in which the student engages; and to what groups (e) in the community and/or in school the student belongs as a participant.

5. A: The only true statement about the CBCL is (a). The information about the child's behavior is reported by the parents. The CBCL does not assess social competencies (b). 118 CBCL items consider possible behavior problems and 20 to social competencies such as school functioning, friendships, group memberships, recreational activities, work activities, and so forth. This instrument can be self-administered by the parent(s) or administered by an interviewer (c). This checklist is standardized and cannot be individualized (d). The CBCL has a standardized format based on empirical research and has norms based on a sample of 1,300 children's parent responses which was found to be representative of the population. The CBCL is not designed for pre-school and elementary school students only (e); it is designed for use with children aged 4 to 18.

6. C: The History/Transition Information Profile would be most useful for a teacher with a class of all new students who have past school records. This instrument helps teachers to learn each student's educational history by offering information about the student's abilities, interests, strengths and weaknesses, and which educational strategies and methods have worked or failed previously. "Step-up" teachers (a) and teachers with mixed-age classes who teach the same students for several years in a row (b) are less likely to need this tool after their first year with students. Teachers with all new students who have no earlier school records (d) would be less able to make use of this transition instrument. They could only use the section "from the family's perspective" to gather information from parents as well as pertinent medical records. Since the teachers described in (c) would benefit most from this instrument, answer (e), all could benefit equally, is incorrect.

7. A: Alfred Binet published the first working intelligence test in France in 1905. Lewis Terman (b) of Stanford University adapted Binet's test for American children in 1916, standardized the test's administration, and later developed age-level norms. Terman's adaptation of Binet's test is called the Stanford Revision of the Binet - Simon scale. David Wechsler (c) published the Wechsler-Bellevue (for Bellevue Hospital in New York, where Wechsler worked) Intelligence Scale in 1939, adding nonverbal as well as verbal measures. It was renamed the Wechsler Adult Intelligence Scale (WAIS) in 1955. Wechsler later created the Wechsler Intelligence Scale for Children (WISC) and the Wechsler Preschool and Primary Scale of Intelligence (WPPSI) to evaluate different age groups. Raymond Cattell (d) created the Culture-Fair (or Culture-Free) Intelligence Test in 1949; in 1963 he identified the distinction between crystallized intelligence and fluid intelligence. Howard Gardner

(e) of Harvard University conceived his theory of multiple intelligences in 1983, identifying eight types of intelligence and later adding a ninth.

8. E: The TAT or the Thematic Apperception Test is a projective test used for personality assessment. The test taker is given ambiguous pictures to view and asked to make up a narrative of what s/he perceives the picture is about. The ITBS (a) or the Iowa Test of Basic Skills, the CTBS (b) or Comprehensive Test of Basic Skills, the SAT (c) or Stanford Achievement Test, and the CAT (d) or California Achievement Test, are all standardized achievement tests. These are normed tests commonly given annually to entire classes of students in elementary and secondary schools. Students' scores are compared to national standards. Results typically give age and grade equivalents for a student's scores, based on national averages.

9. B: The Digit Span subtest of the WISC evaluates short-term or working memory by asking the child to repeat a numbers series after hearing it spoken. Repetition may be in the same order or, in a harder exercise, in reversed order. The Vocabulary (a) subtest measures verbal comprehension (understanding of words) by asking the child to define given words. The Block Design (c) subtest is designed to assess perceptual reasoning ability by asking the child to assemble blocks to match an example given. The Symbol Search (d) subtest which involves matching symbols from rows to target symbols given, measures processing speed. The Picture Concepts (e) subtest is a perceptual reasoning measure (like the Block Design) and asks the child to identify matching pictures from different rows of pictures.

10. D: Being able to follow specific, step-by-step directions is not an executive function. While an inability to follow step-by-step directions represents cognitive dysfunction, following directives represents micromanagement by the director and thus does not require executive functioning from the child. Executive functions require the child to self-direct and make decisions rather than be directed at every step. Retrieving previously learned material (a), and being able to organize one's work (b) are examples of executive function, as are the ability to decide the importance of items in a group, or to assign them priorities (c), and realistic time management (e). Other executive functions include emotional self-regulation; regulation of processing rate; focusing one's attention on a specific task; sustaining one's attention; making transitions from one thing to another when needed; coming up with strategies for studying, test-taking and the like; knowing how to start an assignment; presenting material in a logical order; and monitoring one's own progress.

11. C: A combination of oral and print language teaching has been found to be most effective for developing phonemic awareness. While the complexities of the relationship between phonemic awareness and the acquisition of reading and writing are not fully understood, the necessity of the former to the success of the latter has been clearly established. Oral language teaching only (a) and print language teaching only (b) have both demonstrated effectiveness in developing phonemic awareness, but using a combination of the two (c) has proven even more effective than either one alone.

12. D: The Peabody Picture Vocabulary is designed for assessing receptive vocabulary and intelligence. It is useful for younger children and those with speech or expressive language deficits as it replaces speaking with pointing at the correct picture in response to words spoken by the tester. It can indicate age/grade intellectual levels if specific deficits in receptive language ability (e.g. Wernicke's aphasia, deafness) are absent, and the student is not an ELL. Social Skills Rating System or SSRS (a) measures Positive Social Behaviors, Problem Behaviors, and Academic Competence as rated by teachers, parents, and other students. It can be used to identify behavior problems and interpersonal skills deficits and to plan interventions. The SIB-R (b) refers to the Scales of Independent Behavior, Revised, which gives a comprehensive assessment of 14 areas of adaptive behaviors and 8 of problem behaviors. The Vineland (c) Adaptive Behavior Scales is often used to diagnose developmental disabilities by measuring areas of essential adaptive behavior, including Communication, Daily Living Skills, Socialization and Motor Skills; it includes a supplementary Maladaptive Behavior Index. The Walker-McConnell (e) Scale of Social Competence and School Adjustment is a screening instrument to identify deficits in children's social skills. It tests adaptive classroom behavior and interpersonal social skills, with versions for elementary school ages and adolescents.

13. A: It is important to assess both a student's intellectual ability and adaptive behavior. Adaptive behavior measures will indicate more about a student's performance, but is not necessarily more important than intellectual ability (b), which indicates degree of competence. Both are needed for a complete picture of the student, and their results do not necessarily match (d). For example, high IQ scores but low school grades can identify problems in any number of areas – learning disabilities, attention deficits, behavior problems, emotional problems, mental illness, ineffective teaching strategies, inappropriate school placement, etc. Low IQ scores with high adaptive behavior ratings can indicate that a child with developmental disabilities is capable of functioning socially and academically at higher levels than might be expected given the IQ scores alone. Neither is more important to assess than the other (e).

14. D: Elementary school students are typically in Erikson's fourth stage of Industry vs. Inferiority. For children aged 6-11, success in performing new skills leads to a sense of competence, while failure leads to a sense of inferiority. The first stage, Trust vs. Mistrust (a), is what infant's experience. When their needs are consistently met, a basic trust in the world results; if their needs are met inconsistently, a sense of mistrust develops. Children aged 2-3 are in the second stage, Autonomy vs. Shame and Doubt (b). Children emerge from complete dependency when independent activities are learned, e.g. toileting. Success results in a sense of autonomy while failure results in shame and doubt. The third stage, Initiative vs. Guilt (c), manifests in ages 3-5. Preschoolers actively explore their environment, experimenting with asserting control over it. Success develops a sense of purpose, while failure engenders guilt. After the stage of Industry vs. Inferiority, adolescents (ages 12-18) enter the fifth stage of Identity vs. Role Confusion (e). Teenagers develop their own identity when successful. When unsuccessful, teens become confused, with an unclear sense of self. The other three of Erikson's eight stages are: Intimacy vs. Isolation in young adulthood, which focuses on relationships; Generativity vs. Stagnation in middle age, which focuses on parenting and work; and Ego Integrity vs. Despair in old age, when one reflects on one's life and feels either satisfaction, wisdom, and peace; or regret, bitterness, and despair.

15. B: Collect information to assess and describe the problem behavior. Immediately following this step, gather information to verify how serious the behavior is (d), because some problem behaviors do not require a full functional behavior assessment. Once the behavior has been identified, teachers and parents should first try standard strategies and methods. If standard measures do not work, next (c) refine the definition of the behavior. For example, the student's team can ask whether the behavior is significantly different from other students'; whether the behavior interferes with learning; whether it's the result of cultural differences; whether it's a safety threat; and whether it will result in disciplinary action if it continues. More than one 'yes' answer indicates the functional behavior assessment should continue.

16. E: Gordon Allport proposed a trait theory of personality. Allport published his research in 1937, 1961, and 1966. Hippocrates (a) posited one of the earliest theories of personality in the fifth century B.C. when he theorized that four "humors" or bodily fluids – blood, phlegm, black bile, and yellow bile, were each associated with a different temperament. In the 2nd century A.D., Galen (b) expanded on Hippocrates' theory by specifying that those dominated by blood had a "sanguine" or cheerful temperament; those dominated by phlegm had a "phlegmatic" or apathetic temperament; those dominated by black bile had a melancholy temperament; and those dominated by yellow bile had an irritable temperament. William Sheldon (c) theorized in 1942 that endomorphs with soft, round body builds were relaxed and sociable; mesomorphs with muscular, rectangular physiques were energetic, brave, and assertive; and ectomorphs, with long, thin, delicate builds were introverted, intellectual, and creative. Frank Sulloway (d) theorized in 1996 that personality is influenced by birth order, claiming that first-born children are more compliant while those born later are more open to novelty and rebellion.

17. B: Psychoticism is not one of the "Big Five." Psychoticism was one of three personality traits posited by Hans Eysenck (1973, 1990), along with neuroticism and extraversion. McCrae and Costa's "Big Five" personality traits are Extraversion; Agreeableness (c); Neuroticism (a); Conscientiousness (d); and Openness to experience (e). Each of these five traits represents not just a quantity but a dimension. An individual's personality can be at either pole of the dimension or anywhere in between along the continuum. For example, someone who is extremely outgoing would be at one end of the Extraversion dimension, while someone who is extremely introverted would be at the other end. After a subject's relative degree of each trait/dimension is ascertained, the five dimensions are combined to yield a more specific description of that individual's personality.

18. C: The correct order of Freud's five stages of psychosexual development is (c). In the Oral stage, birth to 1 year, the infant's erogenous zones are oral – the mouth, lips, and tongue which are used for suckling, and weaning is the major developmental task. The Anal stage, age 2-3, includes the developmental task of toilet training; the erogenous zone is the anus as the child learns to control bowel movements. The Phallic stage, age 4-5, shifts the erogenous zone to the genitals as the child discovers their pleasurable aspects. The primary developmental task in this stage is resolution of the unconscious sexual desire for the opposite-sex parent, and aggression against the same-sex parent. The Latency stage, age 6-12, is when the child's sexuality becomes latent, while she/he learns about social relationships and school work is prioritized; this stage has no erogenous zones, and the development of ego defense mechanisms is the primary task. The Genital stage, age 13-18, revisits the Phallic stage; developing mature sexual intimacy is the primary task. Freud also proposed that adult fixation in any stage (except Latency) produced associated behaviors and personality characteristics.

19. A: Norm-referenced tests such as achievement tests are not used in performance-based assessments. Norm-referenced tests measure product while performance-based assessments evaluate process and product (b). Norm-referenced tests focus on separate skills, and are not integrative (c), which is another characteristic of performance-based assessments. Norm-referenced tests contain objective questions and are not constructed within the context of the class curriculum; therefore they are not authentic (d), another criterion for performance-based assessments. Performance-based assessments provide in-depth evaluations within assessment areas, rather than shallowly covering a broad range of topics (e), while norm-referenced tests evaluate a broad range of skills but do not go in depth. Other performance-based assessment criteria specified by these researchers are that they involve constructed responses and that they require higher-order thinking skills.

20. E: It is not an advantage of curriculum-based assessment (CBA) that it need not be given often. On the contrary, it is an advantage of CBA that it can be administered frequently to maintain ongoing formative assessments of the student's progress. The probes are brief, making it practical (c) in terms of teachers' time and cost effectiveness. Frequent administration is also enhanced by the fact that CBA can detect comparatively small changes (d) over short periods of time. The objective scoring (a) of CBA is another advantage as it eliminates inconsistencies. Research has found that CBA has good validity and reliability (b), two of the most important criteria for all assessment instruments; validity means an instrument tests what it intends to test; reliability, that it can be replicated with consistent results.

21. C: Pretend play games would be most appropriate for a four-year-old. Children 2-7 years old are in Piaget's Preoperational stage. A hallmark of this stage is a developing ability to use symbolic thought, i.e. mental representations of absent objects, as evidenced in the "pretend" play of early childhood. The principles of conservation (a) are understood by the stage of Concrete Operations, from 7-11. Centration, focusing on one aspect of a situation to the exclusion of others, is common in preoperational children. For example, a preoperational child shown liquid poured from a short wide container into a tall thin container believes the taller container holds more. This stage has not developed the logic to recognize the amount is the same, only transferred to a differently shaped container. Preoperational children have achieved object permanence (b) but this answer is not as appropriate as pretend play, which emerges in the preoperational stage. Object permanence is achieved in the Sensorimotor stage, often beginning between the ages of 8 and 12 months. The ability to think logically requires abstract thought, which is reached in the stage of Formal Operations, beginning around 11 years; solving logic problems orally (d) isn't appropriate for a four-year-old.

22. D: These all are the most important criteria for high technical quality of assessments. A test should be valid (a); it measures what it is meant to measure. It should be reliable (b); its results are consistent indices of the skills tested when repeated over time, across different raters, across different items or tasks measuring the same skills. A test should be free from bias (c); any conditions that give unfair advantages or disadvantages to some students over others. Since (d) is correct, answer (e), none of these, is incorrect.

23. B: Rater consistency is not a category of evidence used to confirm test validity, but one of several measures of test reliability. How closely the test's contents match up with the standards (a) supports test validity, as is the relationship of the instrument to other measurements proven to indicate accurately the student's ability or knowledge (c). The degree to which variables that could cause inaccuracy in test results have been reduced during the student response process (d), and how much test reliability, validity, and balance of the assessment among skills, content tested, and breadth and depth of knowledge have been confirmed via the application of statistical methods (e) are also categories concerned with test validity.

24. D: These are all main error sources that affect test reliability. Factors within the particular test being administered (a) such as a lack of consistency across items that test the same skills can cause variation in results, making the test less reliable. Factors in the particular students taking a given test (b) can have an impact on reliability if results vary among students, for example, due to linguistic or cultural differences or disabilities. Factors in scoring (c) can affect test reliability if responses to items are not internally consistent, if there is not consistency among forms of the test, or if there is inconsistency among raters doing the scoring. Since (d) is correct, answer (e), none of these, is incorrect.

25. E: These are all sources of bias in testing. Gender (a) can become a source of bias if test questions emphasize skills in which either girls or boys have less experience. Disability (b) will bias test results if test items do not give all students equal opportunities to demonstrate their proficiency, or if students with disabilities have lacked sufficient accessibility to learn the skills being tested. Language (c) is a source of test bias if the same test and administration are used with students whose competence in the language used varies (e.g., ESL or ELL students taking tests in

English along with students whose first language is English). Geography (d) can introduce bias when there are local or regional variations in schools, student knowledge, traditional practices, or material covered by the test.

26. A: These are all meanings for which the term "ipsative" (literally "of the self") is used. Comparing a new score with scores from previous administrations of the same test (b) is ipsative measurement. Comparing subtests of one test (c), is also ipsative, and can reveal whether the student's abilities are consistent or inconsistent across various skill sets. Another type of ipsative measurement is a statistical comparison of student scores on different scales and equating the score variance (d), called ipsatization. In this method, the average of all scores across scales is subtracted from each individual scale score, removing one degree of freedom and equalizing profiles by locating them around the same middle point. Ipsative measurement can also be done via forced-choice test items as in a Likert type of scale (e). With forced choices, the student may find that neither choice quite represents what the student thinks or feels, but s/he is forced to choose the one that is closest to what the student thinks.

27. C: Versatility is not included in Renzulli's three-ring conception of giftedness. In fact, Renzulli's conception explains lesser degrees of versatility in gifted students in that they can vary their levels of each attribute. This also explains why students are often not gifted across the entire range of academic areas. Renzulli's suggests giftedness is found in the intersection of the three rings of ability (a), most often measured by IQ scores—in Renzulli's theory, gifted students will likely have scores above average, but not necessarily extremely high; creativity (b)—many students may have high IQ scores but are not creative, which can be assessed by measures of divergent thinking, fluid intelligence, etc.; and task commitment, in that a student may have the ability to solve a difficult problem but not the commitment to reaching a solution.

28. B: The incorrect statement is (b). Jackie does not have moderate intellectual disability based on an IQ score of 67. Moderate intellectual disability is associated with IQ scores between 40 and 55, while mild intellectual disability is associated with scores between 55 and 70. Severe intellectual disability is associated with scores between 25 and 40; Johnny is profoundly intellectually disabled (a). Jill's score of 102 places her in the average range of intelligence (c), between 85 and 115. Albert's score of 123 defines his IQ as above average (d), between 115 and 130. While scores of 130-145 are classified as moderately gifted, Gail's score of 154 places her as highly gifted (e), between 145 and 160.

29. A: The range is not a measure of central tendency. It is rather a measure of variability. Measures of variability are statistics showing the distribution of scores around a measure of central tendency. The range is the difference between the highest and lowest numbers in a frequency distribution. The mean (b) is a measure of central tendency and corresponds to the average of a group of scores. The mode (c) is a measure of central tendency and represents the most frequently occurring score in a distribution. The median (d) is the middle score of a distribution.

30. E: The inaccurate statement is (e). No kind of correlation between variables ever indicates that one variable causes the other. Correlation does not indicate or imply causation. Correlation only indicates whether there is a relationship between the variables, and if so, the relative strength of that relationship. A correlation coefficient of 0 indicates no consistent relationship between the variables measured (a). A strong negative correlation indicates an inverse relationship, i.e. the higher the scores for one variable, the lower they will be for the other (b). A strong positive correlation means that if scores on one variable are high they will be high on the other variable as well (c), and if scores on one variable are low they will be low on the other. Correlation coefficients range from -1 to +1, with -1 being a perfect negative correlation and +1 a perfect positive correlation (d). Values between (but not including) -1 and 0 are varying degrees of negative correlations that are not perfect. Values between (but not including) +1 and 0 are varying degrees of positive correlations that are not perfect.

31. B: Statistical significance is not a characteristic of descriptive statistics. Determining whether a difference between mean scores for two samples is a statistically significant difference as opposed to a chance variation is a characteristic of inferential statistics. Measures of central tendency (a), measures of variability around a measure of central tendency (c), correlation coefficients (d) showing if there is a relationship between variables and if so, how strong it is, and frequency distributions (e) showing how often each score occurs in a set of data, are all used in descriptive statistics.

32. A: In experimental research, a chosen independent variable is manipulated by the researcher(s). The purpose is to see whether the manipulation of this independent variable will have an effect on the dependent variable (b). Thus the researchers will not manipulate the dependent variable. A confounding variable (c) is one that interferes with the experiment because it was not introduced by the researchers; it could cause effects upon the dependent variable not caused by manipulation of the chosen independent variable. Therefore researchers seek to eliminate confounding variables.

33. C: For the scenario described, a longitudinal research design would be most appropriate. A longitudinal design studies the same individuals over a span of time, collecting data at given time intervals. A cross-sectional design (a) studies different age groups all at one time. Because it does not involve repeated data collection over a long period of time, it would not show whether gains afforded by the early intervention program were maintained five years later. A cross-sequential design (c) combines aspects of both longitudinal and cross-sectional designs in that different age cohorts are studied at the same time and are also studied repeatedly over time. For example, data from a group of five-year-olds and ten-year-olds taken at the same time and again five years later. While this design has benefits, it would not be useful in this scenario, as only one age group is being studied.

34. E: These are all types of program evaluation approaches identified by Steele. The category of kinds of data and kinds of activities (a) includes models that evaluate programs according to the types of data collected and analyzed, and the types of activities performed within the program being evaluated. The category of evaluation of program parts (b) includes models using the approach of evaluating the individual components of a program. This gives the advantage of identifying whether only certain parts of the program need to be changed as opposed to an overall program evaluation. The category of results: objectives attainment (c) includes models that focus on the results of the program, specifically whether the stated objectives of the program have been met or not. The category of results: outcomes and effects (d) includes models that focus on the results of the program by evaluating what kinds of outcomes and effects the program has produced irrespective of the program objectives.

35. D: It is false that quantitative and qualitative research methods are mutually exclusive. They can be used together in the same program evaluation; this can be an advantage as they have differing strengths and weaknesses and provide different kinds of data. Quantitative methods do make it easier to generalize findings (a) from the samples to the population. Quantitative methods make it easier to summarize findings and compare groups (b) because they use standardized measures, responses of large numbers of people to a limited number of questions or items can be measured, allowing broad sets of findings to be presented concisely. Qualitative methods make it easier to go into greater depth and detail (c), though with a much smaller group of people. The validity of quantitative research depends on how well the instruments used are designed, while the validity of qualitative research depends on the skill of the researchers (e), who actually become the instruments themselves when using qualitative methods of inquiry.

36. B: Problem-solving while important, is a cognitive skill rather than a social one. While all members of a group will need to have problem-solving skills, these are not skills specific to cooperative learning groups because all students need them to learn whether their activities are individualized or group. According to researchers in educational psychology, decision-making (a) is a social skill needed for cooperative learning groups to succeed. Trust-building (c) is a social skill required for small groups since successful interaction requires trust. Communication (d) skills are necessary for a cooperative learning group's members to participate effectively, by expressing ideas and understanding those of others. Conflict management (e) is more significant to a group than to individual learning activities, to resolve interpersonal conflicts within the group. Individuals do not have to resolve interpersonal issues when they are not working cooperatively with others.

37. E: Fostering competition among members is not a condition required for cooperative learning groups to be productive. Such groups, as their name signifies, emphasize cooperation rather than competition. Individualized learning is more likely to encourage competition with other students. Positive interdependence (a) is required for cooperative learning groups, as members succeed or fail together. Face-to-face interaction (b) is a condition for cooperative learning to succeed whereby students support each other's success. Group members teaching one another what they know, explaining problem solutions aloud, checking understanding, discussing what they are learning, and linking current studies to previous ones demonstrate face-to-face interaction. Individual and group accountability (c) are also important. The teacher can observe each member's contribution; test individuals; randomly select members to present work orally; assign members to teach what they have learned to others; and keep group size small for greater individual accountability. Group processing (d) is also a condition for cooperative learning groups. Discussion among members to evaluate goal achievement and productive working relationships; analyzing what member's do that is helpful; and making joint decisions are examples.

38. A: The most correct choice is (a). Vygotsky's scaffolding is support that adults give children as they are learning new skills but have not yet mastered them. As a child becomes more competent at the skill, the adults gradually withdraw this support until the child is able to accomplish the task independently and no longer needs it. It is provided as the child is learning, not in advance of learning something new (b). Vygotsky's concept has nothing to do with building a physical structure for children who cannot stand or walk (c). Because Vygotsky's scaffolding is temporary until the child achieves mastery, it is not provided throughout the lifespan (d). It is provided for a limited time, but this time period is not specified as it is dependent upon when the child reaches mastery, and it is not removed abruptly (e) but gradually.

39. C: A child who is slightly ahead in a certain subject helping another child learn in that subject is an example of Vygotsky's ZPD. Because the two children's learning levels are close, they can relate to one another. The more advanced child can remember what strategies worked at the earlier level, and the less advanced child can identify more with the other child than with an adult who mastered this level of learning long ago. It is common for teachers to assign children exercises just beyond what they have mastered (a); learning would not occur if material had already been mastered; but this is not an example of the ZPD. The ZPD does not mean that children who are at the same level help one another (b). For children to combine their findings (d) is a valuable educational exercise, but not an example of the ZPD. A child moving to the next level of difficulty in learning a new skill (e) can happen with or without the ZPD, but since there is no mention in this choice of another child who is farther along in the process assisting the first child, this is also not an example of the ZPD.

40. D: Answer (d) does not correctly describe one of the points stated by OSERS to clarify IDEA regarding AT. If a student's IEP team determines that the student needs AT for home use to have a FAPE, this must be provided, not just in school. Other points which are correctly described include that the school district must supply AT to a disabled student's family at no charge (a); that the need for AT to assure a FAPE must be decided on a case-by-case basis (b); that a student's Individualized Education Plan (IEP) must include the kind of AT needed as well as how much supportive service (c) for the AT is needed; and that parents are given comprehensive procedural safeguards, including providing AT to the child (e).

41. A: Statement (a) is not correct; Pat and Mia do not both have performance-approach goals. Pat has a performance-approach goal (c) orientation which focuses on seeming more competent than others. Mia's goal orientation is that of a mastery goal (d). This orientation focuses on mastering new skills and information. Mia does not want the highest grade but wants to know everything possible about the subject. The reverse of performance-approach goal orientation is performance-avoidance goal orientation. This orientation focuses on avoiding negative judgment from others. Chris shows a performance-avoidance goal (b); he neither wants to seem more competent by getting the highest grade or to become more competent by mastering a subject, but is concerned with not failing the class and thus being judged incompetent.

42. C: The accurate statement is (c). Courtney and Bert both demonstrate internal loci of control by their comments. Individuals with internal loci of control attribute successes to their own effort, and failures to their own lack of effort, locating the sources of control of their outcomes within themselves. Individuals with more external loci of control attribute successes to good luck, help from others, or a teacher's help, and attribute failures to bad luck, sabotage, or an unfair teacher; locating external sources of control over their outcomes. Britney does not demonstrate internal locus of control (b). Courtney shows more internal locus of control, but Bert does not (c). Ernie shows more external locus of control, blaming his teacher and unfairness, but Courtney does not (d). Neither Britney nor Ernie displays internal locus of control (e) in this example.

43. B: The untrue statement is (b). McClelland and others found that those with a high need for achievement actually do not work harder to achieve their goals. In fact, it was found (Feather, 1961) that those with high n Ach scores were more likely to give up on tasks represented to them as difficult (c). Some researchers think that those with high n Ach scores have a need not only for achievement but also for efficiency, i.e. attaining the desired outcome with the least effort necessary (d). McClelland et al (1976) found that sons with high achievement needs were more likely than those with low n Ach scores to exceed their fathers' employment status (a). In another study, McClelland and Franz (1992) found that children whose parents pressure them to achieve in early childhood by enforcing strict rules for feeding and toilet training were more likely to have high n Ach scores as adults, and earn more than those whose parents did not.

44. D: The factors most predictive of a child's IQ score at age 4 in this study were socioeconomic status and the mother's educational level. These were more predictive than educational level of both parents (e), IQ scores of both parents (a), the mother's IQ score only (b), or the mother's educational level alone without SES (c). Poverty is associated with poor maternal health during pregnancy, which often leads to low birth weights. These are both consistently predictive of lower IQ in the child. Poor children are more often malnourished, making it difficult to concentrate and remember things. Impoverished parents are also likely to have fewer resources at home such as books, computers, educational toys and games. Parents who work long hours, and especially single parents, have less opportunity to play with their children, affording less mental stimulation. All of these factors contribute to lower scores on IQ tests for children of low socioeconomic status. The mother's educational level has more impact on the child's IQ due to the typically greater amount of interaction the mother has with the child.

45. C: Manuel is most likely afraid of speaking out of turn or answering incorrectly, as this could lead to feelings of inadequacy or possible social ridicule from his peers. Manuel is probably comfortable speaking English (a) in school since he was fluent before starting school. There is no indication that the teacher is prejudiced (b), nor that Manuel is any less intelligent than the other students (d). Although cultural differences (e) may influence some of his school behaviors, Manuel was raised in the US, which would blunt any drastic value differences in this particular instance.

46. C: The High School and Beyond survey did not find that tracking reduced achievement differences in students of different socioeconomic status. Instead, it suggests that tracking reinforced inequities that already existed among students of different SES. However, was also found to lessen the preexisting disadvantages in achievement for girls (d) and black students (e). While tracking did not eliminate these inequities, the researchers found that it made them "smaller than they may have otherwise been." Tracking did "partially compensate" female and black high school students for the disadvantages they already experienced. This study also found that being placed in the college track improved students' achievement in mathematics (a) and their probability of graduating high school (b). The researchers concluded that their findings gave "qualified support" for the appropriateness and benefits of tracking.

47. D: It is false that 50% of America's ELL population speaks Spanish as a first language; 70% of ELLs in America spoke Spanish as a first language in 2006. By 2006, the population of ELLs in the US had increased 169% since 1886, while the general school population only increased by 12%; this represents ELL population growth over 14 times as great as general school population growth (a). The ELL population in America as a group speaks more than 400 different languages (b). Current projections are that 30% of school-age children in the US will be ELLs by the year 2015 (c). The largest proportion of ELLs in America is made up of those who immigrated before kindergarten and those born in America to immigrant parents (e). These statistics have significant implications for schools, educators, and school psychologists.

48. B: Keeping furniture setups constant once arranged is not a preventive strategy in providing positive behavioral support for the physical classroom environment. The orientation of furniture, students, and teacher should vary in accordance with the individual classroom activity. Arrangements will be different for small group activities than for whole-class presentations. Tone preventive strategy (e), is guaranteeing students can see and hear presentations, which encourages their attention and diminishes disruption. Keeping areas with high traffic free of congestion (a) facilitates free movement and prevents pushing when the whole class is making a transition. Making sure the teacher can easily see the students (c) is preventive both because it is easier for the teacher to monitor the class and because students are less likely to behave inappropriately when they know they are being watched. Keeping materials and supplies handy (d) cuts down on class disruption and wasted time procuring needed materials allowing more time for teaching and learning. It also makes transitions between subjects smoother.

49. A: Classroom expectations should not be as thorough and detailed as possible. If expectations are too complex students are less likely to remember and comply. The same is true if there are too many (b); the expectations should not exceed three to five items. Expectations should be stated in positive terms (c), i.e. the teacher should communicate what s/he expects the students to do, not what s/he expects them not to do. They should be short, simple, concise statements (d). The teacher must be able to enforce the expectations; if observable behaviors are not used, this may not be possible (e). It would be hard to say a student did not follow class rules or meet class expectations if the teacher could not identify anything extrinsic that the student did or did not do.

50. E: Olweus' BPP does not have school system-level components. Although he describes his program as "a long-term, system-wide program for change," it does not actually include program components identified as school system wide. The four levels are school-level components (a), such as establishing a committee, administering a bullying questionnaire school-wide, holding meetings, introducing school rules against bullying, involving the parents, etc.; individual-level components (b), such as supervising student activities, intervening in bullying, meeting with students and parents, and developing individual intervention plans for students involved in bullying; classroom-level components (c), i.e. posting and enforcing school anti-bullying rules, holding regular class meetings and meeting with parents; and community-level components (d), i.e. involving members of the community in the bullying prevention committee, partnering with community members to support the school's program, and aiding in disseminating best practices principles and anti-bullying messages in the community.

51. D: High school is the level that the Olweus program was not specifically researched and designed for, but some high schools have still used the program to address bullying as it is very effective. In addition, many schools have used this program for kindergarten classes. The program was researched at and designed for elementary (a), middle (b), and junior high schools (c).

52. E: More students from all of these categories are in schools today than in the past, creating a greater need for school safety programs. Students from dysfunctional families (a) are more likely to display dysfunctional behavior their families have modeled and are at higher risk for disruptive behaviors in school; those who are not disruptive are at higher risk for failing academically and socially because of emotional problems created by their home lives. Students from impoverished families (b) are at greater risk for poorer academic performance. Also, the pressure created by poverty can contribute to crime in schools, such as stealing and drug trafficking. Students with teenage parents (c) are at risk due to teens' generally less adequate parenting skills, lack of experience, emotional immaturity, lack of resources, and greater need for support services in parenting. Students requiring special education (d) are increasingly mainstreamed into regular public schools today, making it harder for schools to have adequate resources to serve them, as is true with all of these groups.

53. C: Being models of pro-social behavior equally as teaching school subjects would not be a goal for school administrators, but rather a goal for teachers in implementing a safe-school plan. Educators state that teachers should regard modeling pro-social behaviors for students as just as important as teaching academic subjects. Goals for school administrators in implementing a safe-school plan include (a) providing leadership in developing the plan, monitoring it and evaluating it; (b) creating a program wherein they can continually track school crime, report it, give feedback on it, and communicate this information to those concerned; (d) designing the school's environment to assure that traffic to, from and within the schools is kept safe; and (e) setting up procedures for crisis management when needed and for evacuation in case of emergencies. Another goal for administrators in a safe-school program is creating a school planning team or safety council to advise and decide about school crime cases, assess the safety of the school, and propose changes to the safety plan and code of discipline as needed.

54. E: All of these should be included (e). To ensure the most balanced input to a school safety council, representatives should include members of the school staff (a), students themselves (b), parents of students attending that school (c), and representatives from the community (d). All of these individuals offer differing perspectives. It The social interactions contributing to school crime are complex and involve multiple sources; representing a variety of positions is essential. It is also important to see that all of the parties named are informed of and agree to school safety policies and procedures in order to enforce them.

55. A: Answer (a) is not correct. ABA has actually been found to be effective in classroom learning as well as the other areas described. Since its inception, Skinnerian behavior analysis has grown in its application until currently it is found to have a very broad range of areas in which it proves effective. Many prefer it as treatment for behavior problems related to intellectual disability (b), and autism spectrum disorders (c), in which it has been found to revolutionize the field, as well as for brain injuries (d).

56. B: Conducting clinical therapy 1:1 with individual students is an inappropriate activity for a school counselor. This should be done by a clinical psychologist. It is appropriate for school counselors to help individual students plan their academic programs (a); to do group counseling with small or large groups of students (c); to counsel students who have disciplinary problems (d); and attending students' IEP (individualized education program) meetings to advocate for them (e). School counselors can also interpret students' aptitude tests, achievement tests, cognitive tests and school records; make sure student records are maintained according to government regulations; analyze students' grades relative to achievement; counsel students on attendance and dress issues; work with teachers to present guidance curriculum lessons; give teachers recommendations for study hall management; helping the principal to identify and resolve student issues; and analyzing disaggregated data.

57. D: It is false that federal law dictates that each field has separate and exclusive programs. Federal laws (i.e. ADA and IDEA) dictate inclusion of students with disabilities, requiring that early childhood education and special education programs collaborate; their programs must interact, coordinate, and complement one another. Both of these fields stress the importance of individualized interventions and programs (a) to address the particular child's needs. Both fields agree that assessment needs to be multidimensional and naturalistic (b). For example, using the results of just one test to qualify a child for special education or to justify grade retention is rejected by both fields. Both disciplines also find that for all children, learning must be personally relevant (c). Children learn better when the materials and topics involved have personal meaning for them.

58. C: Taking charge is not one of the things recommended in conflict resolution for children. Children must work together to resolve conflict (d); having them all trying to take control would produce more conflict. Children are advised to first understand (a) what the conflict is about by allowing each child to express feelings in turn while the others listen without interrupting. Children are then advised to avoid making things worse (b) by steering clear of insults, telling secrets or dredging up past events, shouting, and physical aggression. Next, children are advised to work together (d) by using "I" statements to avoid blame and take responsibility; to take turns talking; to maintain quiet voices; to write down their perception of the problem and read what others wrote; and to use active listening techniques. Finally, they will seek the solution (e), through group brainstorming, and if needed, enlist someone outside the group to write down the ideas and suggest ways of making the group's ideas workable, or to provide a different perspective.

59. B: According to the CMI's training, the classroom is not a level at which crisis planning takes place. It is done at the building (a) level, typically the first level after a crisis is reported and involves such things as verifying information, informing district administrators and affected staff, delegating responsibilities and defining roles, use of support personnel, managing or changing routines, etc. It is addressed on the district level (c) to decide how crisis response team members will be shared among buildings, select team members not emotionally involved, and ensure all members have equivalent training. Since substitutes must be hired when response team members are teachers, the school board needs to approve the costs involved. On the team level (d), planning includes deciding who to contact first, notifying response team members, hiring substitutes when needed, annual training as members leave and are replaced, regular mini-trainings, regularly updating crisis response plans, and creating handouts. At the community level (e), communities contribute resources, coordinating existing resources and creating new ones as needed. A community crisis response team can include 911 emergency personnel, juvenile department personnel, mental health personnel, parents, representatives of minority groups, hospital social workers, hospice workers, funeral home personnel, businesses, service groups, and so on depending on the nature of the crisis.

60. A: All of these are school climate assessment instruments. The Education, Training, Research Character Education Survey (b) from ETR Associates has student and staff versions, with overlapping items so they may be compared. It has scales on sense of community, bonding with school, school values, student behavior, adult behavior, and intergroup relations. The Tribes Assessment Questionnaire (c) is a survey from Center Source Systems which can be filled out by students, parents, teachers, staff, and administrators. It has scales on caring and compassion, responsibility, justice and fairness, trustworthiness, honesty, doing one's personal best, and social skills. The CASE-1987 (d) is the Comprehensive Assessment of School Environments from the National Association of Secondary School Principals. In addition to a school climate survey, it includes surveys of student, teacher, and parent satisfaction. Its school climate survey includes subscales on teacher-student relationships, security and maintenance, administration, student academic orientation, student behavioral values, guidance, student-peer relationships, parent and community-school relationships, instructional management, and student activities. The SCCP-2000 (e) is the School as Caring Community Profile from SUNY Cortland. It has subscales on perceptions of student respect, perceptions of student friendship and belonging, perceptions of students' shaping of their environment, perceptions of support and care by and for faculty/staff, and perceptions of support and care by and for parents.

61. A: Cystic Fibrosis is a genetic disease, and is not in the DSM-5. The Diagnostic and Statistical Manual of Mental Disorders, fifth edition (DSM-5, 2013) includes clinical disorders such as schizophrenia (ICD-10 code F20.9). It also includes personality disorders such as antisocial personality disorder (F60.2), and developmental disorders such as speech sound disorder (F80.0). Developed by the American Psychiatric Association, the DSM-5 is the most generally utilized classification system in the United States for psychological disorders.

62. C: Part of being a professional involves identifying gaps in one's knowledge and attempting to fill them in the best possible way. Of the options mentioned, taking a seminar would provide professional leadership, a clear curriculum, and other students for feedback. Earning a certificate would also boost the attendee's confidence that, on completing the course, he has gained the diagnostic skills needed to succeed in his work. Asking a colleague for advice (a) could be useful but will not provide all the knowledge necessary. Reading the entire DSM-5 document (b) would also be useful, but would take a long time and might not focus on the immediately practical things. Putting off the paperwork (d) or choosing not to use the new DSM (e) are not solutions to the problem.

63. B: Although the DSM is an American invention, issues of mental health are of worldwide concern. With the country's engagement in ongoing war scenarios, more veterans than ever are experiencing physical and mental trauma on battlefields far from home during their service as well as after being demobilized. Refugees are another concern; the organizations that deal with worldwide crisis, such as the Red Cross and the World Health Organization can eliminate some confusion in communications by speaking the same psychological language. By adding the WHODAS to the DSM-5, the authors have taken an important first step in integrating American psychological diagnostics with those of the larger world. The GAF has been removed from the DSM-5 (a), (d). While the transition away from the axis system of classification (e) may be a good change, it is not related to global healthcare.

64. B: The least likely indication of substance abuse is that the student tells you about personal problems. Students abusing drugs are more likely to share few personal issues or none at all. According to the Centers for Disease Control, a sudden, sharp drop in grades (a) is a warning sign of substance abuse because it interferes with attention, concentration, memory, ability to study, and motivation. Students also often lose interest in school subjects when they are abusing drugs. Sudden truancy or increased unexplained absences (c) is identified as a warning sign of substance abuse. The cognitive and physiological impairments caused by drugs can interfere with attendance. Depending on the drug of choice, they may also lose track of time and actually forget to go to school if their consciousness is altered enough. Or they may sleep all day recovering from the effects of alcohol, opiates, or stimulants. If a student loses interest in what have been favorite subjects (d), this is another warning sign of substance abuse. Sufficiently severe abuse may result in loss of interest in anything. Another warning sign of substance abuse is if a student's attention span and memory decrease noticeably (e). Inability to sustain one's attention or to remember things can both be induced by the use and/or abuse of substances.

65. C: If behavior problems are serious enough, any of these would warrant requesting a behavioral consultation. The student's individual diagnosis is not the criterion for determining such a request, but the seriousness of problem behaviors resulting from the disorder or disturbance. If the behaviors are disruptive to learning, pose a threat to safety, cause physical harm, and/or have not responded to interventions already known and available within the school, behavioral consultation is indicated. Some students with autism (a) can engage in serious problem behaviors, especially when frustrated by changes without adequate transitions, an inability to communicate verbally, or as a reaction to sensory stimuli. Students with bipolar disorder (b) are subject to mood swings from mania to depression, especially if they are unmedicated or the medication is not effective. Severely bipolar individuals can suffer from delusions and/or hallucinations, resulting in unpredictable behavior; and severe depression can lead to suicidal behavior. Students with ADHD (d) cannot learn if their attention deficit is severe enough, and hyperactive behavior can be extremely disruptive to others. Emotionally disturbed students (e) may or may not exhibit very disruptive behavior in school. However, students who are not disruptive may still need behavioral consultation since their emotional disturbance can result in other behaviors, such as failing to attend class, study or do homework.

66. A: It is false that mental health consultants in early childhood programs do not conduct direct therapeutic interventions. MH consultants use play therapy and/or other developmentally appropriate therapeutic interventions with the children as indicated. One role of MH consultants in early childhood programs is to give information, instruction, and support to teachers and administrators to help them deal more effectively with children with problem behaviors or developmental delays (b). Another is to consult with teachers or case management teams to resolve problems with an individual child and/or family (c). Yet another role of MH counselors in early childhood programs is to coach parents on ways to interact more effectively with their children when they are at home (d). MH consultants in early childhood programs can also help families to access and use MH services outside of their program for diagnosis and treatment (e).

67. D: According to UM's lab for IC teams, the goal of IC teams is to enhance, improve, and increase the performance of students and staff. Goals are more global while objectives are specific instances of how to achieve that goal. The objectives of IC teams according to the UM lab are: (a) to establish a systematic network of support, to include a trained IC team, in every building; (b) to improve or enhance teachers' skills in and use of instructional best practices in both assessment and delivery; (c) to develop norms to be used throughout the school for collaborating and solving problems; and (e) to make effective use of data to inform decisions made in the classroom and the school.

68. C: According to the Indiana School Boards Association, the incorrect statement is that (c) school board policies should tell administrators how to do what they should do. School board policies should tell school administrators what they should do (b), but not how they should do it. Policy helps to guide decisions and should be clear, but is written in general terms. This allows administrators to choose their own methods for accomplishing what policy requires. School board policies should give schools a definite course of action to pursue (a). In some cases, these policies have been dictated by laws (d). In other cases, policies are dictated by obvious common sense (e).

69. B: The hippocampus is the largest structure in the limbic system and has the most involvement of the structures listed here in forming new explicit memories. The hypothalamus (a) regulates motivated behavior such as eating and drinking, maintains homeostasis, or internal equilibrium, and regulates the actions of the endocrine system. The cerebellum (c) coordinates body movements, controls body posture, and maintains the body's equilibrium or balance. It is also involved in the learning and performance of sequences of body movements. The amygdala (d) regulates emotional states, aggression, and the acquisition of emotional memory. The thalamus (e) is the structure in the brain that sends sensory impulses to the cerebral cortex for processing.

70. A: Although no one lobe of the brain exclusively controls any one function, the most likely lobe to be damaged when these problems exist is the frontal lobe. The frontal lobe, at the front of each hemisphere, is involved in cognitive functions such as planning, making decisions, and setting goals, and controls motor functions. The parietal lobe (b), at the upper side of each hemisphere, handles the sensations of touch, temperature, and pain, so problems with the executive functions described would not be attributable to parietal lobe damage. The temporal lobe (c), at the lower side of each hemisphere handles the hearing process; no executive functions occur there. The occipital lobe (d) controls visual processes and would not be the area damaged if executive cognitive functions are impaired. For all four lobes (e) to be damaged would be unlikely in this case. If there were such widespread damage, this student would have more problems than just with the functions described.

71. C: It is not true that neither emotional reactivity nor environmental stressors were found to affect schizophrenia symptoms. Researchers (Docherty et al, 2008) found that schizophrenics had increased delusions and hallucinations in the presence of both high emotional reactivity and stressful life events. Neither those that had more intense emotional reactions but no stressful events in their lives, nor had those who experienced environmental stressors but had lower emotional reactions increased symptoms. Only those with both showed increases in symptoms over a nine-month period. Research by Gottesman (1991) found that while the risk of schizophrenia in the general population was 1%, the risk for children whose parents both had schizophrenia was 46% (a), and also that the probability of identical twins having schizophrenia was around three times higher than for fraternal twins (b). Barkataki et al (2006) found through magnetic resonance imaging (MRI) schizophrenics often have larger ventricles (channels that cerebrospinal fluid flows through) in their brains than do normal brains (d). Kuperberg et al (2003) found that schizophrenics had thinner areas in the frontal and temporal lobes of their cerebral cortex, indicating loss of brain tissue. Thompson et al (2001) found that the brains of schizophrenic adolescents lost considerably more gray matter over five years (e) than the brains of healthy adolescents.

72. E: Research has identified all of these as factors associated with higher rates of schizophrenia. People who live in cities (a) have higher rates than those in rural or suburban areas. People with financial problems (b) experience higher rates of schizophrenia than those with fewer or no money problems. People who have emigrated from one country to another (c) demonstrate higher rates of diagnosed schizophrenia than those who did not migrate. People who experienced traumatic events (d) such as physical or sexual abuse show increased probabilities of suffering from schizophrenia. These findings show that in addition to genetic factors, environmental factors also influence schizophrenia, so both nature and nurture are involved.

73. A: A student with Wernicke's aphasia will have difficulty understanding what you say. Damage to Wernicke's area in the temporal lobe interferes with receptive language, the ability to process spoken language. Those with Wernicke's aphasia can speak fluently (b), but don't understand what is being said. Because they never understand both parts of conversations, eventually what they say has increasingly less meaning. They may speak logically in response to visual stimuli. Many patients with this disorder hide it by developing stock expressions; for example, if asked a question they may respond "How nice you look today!" or "Is it still raining out?" While irrelevant to the conversation, they make sense on their own and can distract you from your question. Wernicke's aphasia is not associated with deafness (c); but is an inability to process spoken language and understand meaning. Such individuals have no difficulty with spelling and grammar (d) if they did not have trouble with them before the aphasia.

74. D: A short attention span is not a common characteristic of autism spectrum disorders, but of attention deficit disorders. Many students with autistic disorders focus on one activity for long periods, and tend to have a very narrow range of solitary interests as they have difficulty with social interactions (b). Their intense focus on an activity is not easily disrupted; hence they need sufficient transition from one activity to the next. They require rigid routines and can become upset if these are changed (e). Psychologists have theorized that autistic children have difficulty with social interaction because they cannot understand others' feelings (c). According to researchers, autistic children do not form the "theory of mind" that other children do at young ages—the understanding that others have different points of view. Recent research indicates that autistic individuals can learn to identify social cues such as facial expressions which they otherwise cannot interpret. Neuropsychologists believe that such training rewires the brain, bypassing dysfunctional areas. Autistic individuals frequently engage in repetitive and ritualistic behaviors (a), such as arranging objects in symmetrical patterns, which are soothing activities. Autistics also commonly display hypersensitivity to sensory stimuli—sounds are too loud, lights and colors too bright, scratchy clothes painful. The combination of sensory hypersensitivity and difficulty with social activities means that situations with noisy crowds are very stressful for them and may precipitate behavioral problems.

75. B: The only correct statement with reference to Pavlov's classical conditioning is (b). The food was an unconditioned stimulus; no learning or conditioning was required to elicit the response of salivation in Pavlov's dogs; salivation was automatic. (a) The food was not an unconditioned stimulus, nor was the tone paired with the introduction of food (c) because it did not cause salivation by itself. But once the dogs had been repeatedly exposed to the tone accompanying food, they salivated at the sound because they associated it with food. The tone then became a conditioned stimulus. It is false that salivation was always an unconditioned response (d) or always a conditioned response (e). It was both at different times in the experiment.

76. C: It is false that classically conditioned and operant responses are elicited by particular stimuli. Operants (behaviors emitted by an organism that affect, or operate on, the environment) are not elicited by certain stimuli. Operant conditioning can increase or decrease the probability of an operant behavior recurring in the future by manipulating its consequences (d). In other words, changing what happens following the behavior (the consequence) will cause the organism to do it more or less. If a child does something and receives a reward immediately afterward, the child is more likely to do that thing again. Rewards are called reinforcement because they reinforce the probability that the behavior will be repeated. If a child does something and the behavior either receives punishment or is ignored (extinction), the likelihood that the child will repeat the behavior is diminished. It is true that classical conditioning was developed earlier than operant conditioning (a). Pavlov began his experiments in classical conditioning in the late 1920s and Skinner began his experiments in operant conditioning in the 1960s. It is true that operant conditioning involves voluntary behaviors and classical conditioning involves involuntary ones (b). Classical conditioning conditions reflex behaviors to occur in the presence of previously neutral stimuli while operant conditioning changes the frequency of behaviors that are not automatic.

77. A: Psychologist G. Stanley Hall is the only researcher listed who viewed adolescence as a period of "storm and stress" (1904). Cultural anthropologists (b) Margaret Mead (1928) and (c) Ruth Benedict (1938) studied different cultures in which adolescents did not seem to experience any major upheaval but gradual transitions instead. More recent research by (d) psychologist Jeffrey J. Arnett (1999) confirms that the adolescent experience varies according to culture.

78. B: This example illustrates displacement. Displacement is releasing pent-up feelings – usually of hostility – onto someone or something less threatening than the original cause. The teacher is an adult authority figure, so Charlie could not yell back at her. But his little sister is not a threat to him, so he took out his anger at the teacher on her, which was safer. Projection (a) is attributing one's own impulses to others or blaming them for one's own problems. A man that desires a woman who rejects him might insist that she wants him. Regression, (c), is reverting to an earlier developmental level. Children who envy all the attention a new baby is getting may regress to babyish behavior in an attempt to compete. Sublimation, (d), is channeling unacceptable impulses into socially acceptable activities. Random aggression is not acceptable in society, but becoming a professional boxer or wrestler can channel aggressive impulses into acceptable forms. Reaction formation, (e), is reacting against threatening inner impulses by forming behaviors or attitudes opposite to those impulses. People who are afraid of their own sexual urges and engage in reaction formation might become extremely prudish and condemn sexual activity.

79. E: The theory of Carl Rogers is not a cognitive theory of personality but a humanistic theory of personality. Humanistic theories are phenomenological, emphasizing the individual's subjective point of view and the also the need for self-actualization or realizing one's potential. Rogers pioneered person-centered or client-centered therapy and emphasized the importance of unconditional positive regard by parents in child rearing and by therapists in counseling. The social learning theory of Albert Bandura (a) is a cognitive theory. Bandura pioneered the concept of self-efficacy, or the belief that one has the competence to perform successfully in a given situation; the concept of reciprocal determinism, meaning that the individual and the environment mutually affect one another; and the concept of observational or vicarious learning, meaning that an individual can learn by observing others' experiences without having to have the experience directly oneself. The cognitive-affective personality theory of Walter Mischel (b) emphasizes the understanding of behavior as a function of interactions between persons and situations. He defined variables, such as encodings; expectancies and beliefs; affects; goals and values; and competencies and self-regulatory plans, which determine how a person will behave in given situations. The social intelligence theory of Nancy Cantor (c) is a cognitive theory of personality. She defined three dimensions of individual differences: choice of life goals; knowledge relevant to social interactions; and strategies for implementing goals. According to Cantor, these three interact to form the different behavior patterns that form personality. The expectancy theory of Julian Rotter (d) is a cognitive theory of personality. Expectancy is how much we believe our behaviors will bring rewards. Rotter identified locus of control, or how much we attribute events to what we do (internal) or to the environment (external).

80. D: Socialism is not one of Batson's motivations for pro-social behavior. Socialism is a group of theories of social, political, and economic organization. Altruism (a), or acting for the benefit of others, is one of the motivations Batson identified. Egoism (b), or helping others to benefit oneself, is another. Some people will help others in exchange for a return favor or to receive a reward. Collectivism (c), or helping for the benefit of a group such as a family, a political party, or an organization, is a third motivation proposed by Batson. Principlism (e), or helping others to fulfill a moral, civic, or religious principle, is a fourth motive that Batson named.

81. A: Spearman and Gardner formed, respectively, the most reductionist and most expansionist theories of intelligence. Charles Spearman (1927) theorized a factor of general intelligence called g that underlies all intelligence performance. He also identified domain-specific skills, or s; s is less a separate type of intelligence as a group of specific subsets of abilities related to areas of knowledge while g still underlies all intelligent performance. Howard Gardner (1999, 2006) formulated a theory of multiple intelligences, expanding the definition of intelligence beyond the measurements of IQ tests. He defined eight types of intelligence, later adding a ninth. Raymond Cattell and Robert Sternberg (b) fall in the middle. Cattell (1963) used factor analysis to conclude that Spearman's idea of general intelligence could be divided into two independent parts: crystallized intelligence and fluid intelligence. Crystallized intelligence is learned knowledge together with the individual's ability to retrieve that information. This component of intelligence enables management of concrete and routine or recurrent tasks in life. Fluid intelligence is the ability to solve problems and identify complex relationships, and permits addressing abstract and novel tasks. Robert Sternberg (1999) formulated the triarchic theory of intelligence. Analytical intelligence provides information-processing abilities needed to problem-solve familiar tasks. Creative intelligence is the ability to solve novel or unfamiliar problems. Practical intelligence is tied to specific contexts and allows adaption to various contexts, select appropriate ones, and shape the environments to meet needs.

82. D: Noam Chomsky is not known for subscribing to the idea of linguistic relativity. Chomsky postulated the existence of a language acquisition device (LAD) he said was inherent in all humans irrespective of teaching or other environmental factors. He also theorized a universal grammar, an innate body of linguistic knowledge. Edward Sapir (a) proposed that differences in languages create differences in thought, a radical concept at the time. Benjamin Whorf (b) was a student of Sapir's. They studied different cultures and concluded that the language people speak influences how they think. For example, people of the Dani culture in Papua New Guinea have two words for colors meaning black/dark and white/light, while English uses eleven basic color terms. Sapir and Whorf are known for their principle of linguistic relativity. Based on the Sapir-Whorf Hypothesis, as the linguistic relativity principle is often known, Roger Brown (c) distinguished between weak linguistic relativity, wherein language limits thought, and strong linguistic relativity, wherein language determines thought. Since (d) Chomsky is not known to subscribe to linguistic relativity, answer (e), all of these are, is incorrect.

83. E: These all represent limitation in self-report measures. Children too young for speech, deaf and some autistic individuals, others who are nonverbal, and students with delayed and/or limited language development (a) cannot respond to written surveys or oral interviews as others can. Some people with mental illnesses (b) may be unable to understand and/or respond appropriately to self-report measures; for example, those with disorganized thinking, delusions, hallucinations, and other symptoms can have altered perceptions of reality and/or disordered expressive language.

Validity of the measurement (c) can be questionable as respondents may misunderstand questions, inaccurately remember what they are to report, give untrue or misleading responses manipulatively, be embarrassed to tell the truth about some items, or may lie to meet some end, such as to be hired by an employer or to released from a mental hospital. These factors will also affect reliability (d) if the respondent answers differently at another time when situations have changed. Reliability is also affected in interviews if the interviewer is biased and this affects the way s/he asks questions and the way they are answered.

84. C: Jean Piaget made extensive use of naturalistic observation of children in the research that formulated his theory of cognitive development. He unobtrusively observed the behavior of children as they played, exploring and acting on their environment, so as not to influence their behaviors. He also used case studies to develop thorough profiles of the individual children he studied. Sigmund Freud (a), the father of psychoanalysis and psychiatry, primarily used interviews, free association, and dream interpretation and analysis to formulate his psychoanalytic theory. He did not observe people in their natural settings but rather asked them questions and/or listened to them talk in his office. B. F. Skinner (b), pioneer of behavior modification through operant conditioning, originally experimented with animals in his laboratory, manipulating the consequences of their behaviors to change the probability of those behaviors in the future. He used operant chambers or "Skinner boxes" and other devices. He later worked with humans as well, but he still manipulated consequences to increase or decrease the probability of their engaging in certain behaviors. His purpose was see how he could change behavior by manipulating conditions in a lab setting, not to observe the subjects in their natural settings. Since (c) Piaget is the only correct answer, answer (d), all of these, and answer (e), none of these, are both incorrect.

85. B: A student with Broca's aphasia can be expected to have trouble expressing themselves in words. This type of aphasia involves damage to Broca's area, a part of the brain in the left hemisphere discovered by Paul Broca that is responsible for the processing of expressive language. Individuals with this disorder have difficulty retrieving words they already know, hampering their expression as they struggle to find words they cannot locate to communicate with others. They can also have difficulty ordering words into sentences and other functions of expressive language. Because Broca's aphasia is a disorder of expressive language, it does not normally affect receptive language, so those with Broca's aphasia can understand what you say to them (a). A disorder of receptive language is Wernicke's aphasia, which affects Wernicke's area, the part of the brain responsible for processing the spoken language that is heard. A student with Broca's aphasia would not have trouble understanding what she sees (c). Such a problem would be related to damage in the occipital lobe, which processes visual information. A student who has problems with motor coordination (d) is more likely to have damage in the cerebellum, which is responsible for motor coordination, balance or equilibrium, and body position or posture.

86. A: Content validity means that a test measures the complete range of the domain being tested. For example, testing students on their satisfaction with school would not provide information about their satisfaction with life; that would require testing their satisfaction with family, friendships outside school, leisure activities, etc. Criterion validity (b) means that a test's results correlate positively with another criterion for what the test measures. A student's scores on an achievement test that correlate highly with the student's class grades, indicates criterion validity, with grades being the criterion. Criterion-referenced tests employ this principle. Predictive validity (c) is simply another term for criterion validity. Construct validity (d), as its name implies, means that a test does a good job of measuring the construct underlying it. For example, such abstract qualities as anxiety, depression, or aggression do not have a single perfect criterion, so psychologists create constructs, or theories, about them. A test will have construct validity if its scores correlate highly with validated measures of the characteristics used to define the construct.

87. C: Split-half reliability is one measure of internal consistency, which is a measure of reliability related to the degree of consistency of the responses within one test. This can be demonstrated by comparing a student's scores on odd-numbered items with scores on even-numbered items; this is called split-half reliability. Split-half reliability is not measured using parallel test forms (a); these are different versions of a test. Using parallel forms is another way to evaluate a test's reliability as it mitigates a practice effect in students who take the identical form of a test repeatedly and may remember items. In the case of survey questionnaires asking for opinions, where there are no correct or incorrect answers, parallel forms can also decrease the effects of a respondent's wish to demonstrate consistent responses to the same items over repeated administrations. Split-half reliability is not an indicator of test-retest reliability (b). Test-retest reliability measures of how highly the scores correlate between two different administrations of the same test to the same individuals; people who got the highest and lowest scores the first time will do so the second time if there is good test-retest reliability. The higher the correlation coefficient between the two administrations of the test, the more reliable the test is.

88. D: The researchers concluded that this discrepancy was due to an unfair cultural bias in the test's items. To privileged White children, social conventions taught that a cup and saucer went together. But poorer Black children's families typically did not have sets of china with cup-and-saucer pairs. In their homes, a cup was simply set on the table. Thus, for their cultural background, their choice of "table" as the correct answer was logical. This revelation prompted the development of "culture-free" or "culture-fair" tests, such as Cattell's, as well as a test specifically oriented to black culture by Robert L. Williams, Ph.D., which he jocularly named the B.I.T.C.H test: Black Intelligence Test of Cultural Homogeneity. It contains items such as "Deuce-and-a-quarter is: (a) money; (b) a car; (c) a house; (d) dice;" the correct answer is (b) a car—deuce-and-a-quarter was black slang for the Oldsmobile 225, a luxury model auto. Williams called attention to the cultural bias in favor of whites by turning it on its head with this test. Hence the Black children's incorrect answers on the white-designed test were not due to cognitive impairment (a), inadequate vocabularies (b), or disparity in intelligence between the races (c).

89. B: It is not one of the general principles under the Professional Competency section of the Principles for Professional Ethics of the NASP (National Association of School Psychologists)'s Professional Conduct Manual for School Psychology not to inform clients of their education and experience. One general principle is to represent competence levels, training, education, and experience accurately to clients in a professional manner. Another is to (a) recognizing the strengths and limitations of one's training and experience. Psychologists should not undertake practices unless qualified, or they should seek referrals to, consultation with, or supervision by other specialists as needed. Another general principle is (c) not using their affiliations with individuals, professional organizations, or universities and other institutions, to over-represent their levels of competence. Pursuing continuing professional development to stay current in their field (d) is another of these general principles. The last principle is (e), not allowing personal problems or conflicts to compromise professionalism, and if there are conflicts in professional relationships, to seek qualified assistance in resolving these.

90. E: All of these statements represent additional APA guidelines regarding deception. APA guidelines state that the topics for study and the hypotheses proposed must be found important enough to the advancement of education and science to justify the use of deception (a); that the researchers must show there are no other procedures without deception that will work as well as the procedures involving deception (b); and that after the study is finished, researchers must explain the deception to participants (c). This part of the process is called debriefing. Moreover, APA guidelines specify that once participants are informed about the deception, they have the option to take the data on their own participation out of the study (d) if they are so inclined.

91. D: It is false that the participants were not provided a debriefing following the procedure. Milgram and his team debriefed participants by explaining they were not actually shocking people. By today's APA guidelines, they would not have been allowed to deceive the participants because of significant emotional distress. The participants in these experiments did not go through the current informed consent process (a). Research participants must now be informed about procedures and the risks and benefits of participating, and then sign a document giving their consent to participate. They must also be told they may withdraw from the study at any time with no repercussions. Milgram's researchers repeatedly told participants who complained when they heard screaming that they "must continue" to "shock" the "learners." The procedures in Milgram's experiments would violate today's APA guidelines on deception (b) as well, because participants were misled about the chances of physical or emotional distress being caused by the research, to both the "learners" and to themselves. Milgram's procedures also would not pass the risk/gain assessments mandated today (c), which dictate that risks in any study be minimized, that participants be informed first of the risks, and that appropriate precautions be taken in the event of strong reactions.

92. C: The incorrect statement is (c). School psychologists should discuss recommendations for program changes or additional services, including available alternatives, with the appropriate persons. Moreover, (a) school psychologists' professional practices should always maintain the dignity and integrity of their clients, with sensitivity to the intimacy and confidentiality of such services. School psychologists should explain significant aspects of their professional relationships in a clear, understandable, and age-appropriate way (b). These significant aspects include the reasons services were requested, who will be given information about the services, and what outcomes are possible. These principles also state that school psychologists will respect a child's right to initiate services,* participate in them, or terminate them voluntarily (d). (*The manual states elsewhere that school psychologists must also seek parental support, that children's rights to initiate services without parental consent can vary, and that consequently, the pertinent local, state, and federal laws and ordinances.)

93. B: The incorrect statement is (b). Software publishers are not responsible for ethical/legal use of technology services; the principle states that school psychologists who use the technology services are completely responsible. School psychologists who publicly give lectures, present papers, or publish books or articles should first get written consent or remove identifying data before presenting their work (a). School psychologists should not use computerized test scoring systems unless trained (c). School psychologists should not use technology that ultimately lowers the quality of service (d). Student or client records should never be transmitted electronically unless privacy has been guaranteed (e). This guarantee involves encrypting or removing identifying data from e-mails; requiring that employees working with student/client records be cleared to work with confidential files; and assuring that fax machines receiving confidential files are placed in secure locations.

94. E: This guideline in the NASP manual does not list changing services based on outcome evaluation as one of the purposes of the collaborative decision-making process. It lists the identification of academic and behavior problems (a); the collection and analysis of information for understanding these problems (b); and that a purpose of this process is to aid in making decisions about service delivery (c), e.g. what kinds of services should be provided and how they will be delivered. Another purpose of this process it lists is for evaluating the outcomes of service delivery (d).

95. A: The incorrect statement is (a). School psychologists do not function to maintain the status quo at all levels of the system. A principle of this Practice Guideline is that they function as agents of change at the student, classroom, building, district, local, state, and federal levels. Promoting healthy learning environments by using their skills in conflict resolution (b), and negotiation are other principles of this guideline, as is transmitting information in a relevant, organized way to a large variety of communities (c) composed of parents, teachers, school boards, policy makers, business leaders, and fellow school psychologists. Guideline 2 also states that school psychologists understand and participate in the policy determination process (d). They can promote organizational change and development by applying decision-making strategies to public policy decisions. Another of the five principles under Practice Guideline 2 is that school psychologists have proficiency in systems consultation and decision making (e), and use this skill to encourage collaboration and communication with students, school staff, families, professionals in the community, and agencies.

96. E: Practice Guideline 5 includes all of these principles with respect to diversity. School psychologists design academic and behavioral interventions, understanding that the most effective ones will be tailored to the individual student's qualities and needs (a). They are able to identify subtle biases with regard to race, class, culture, and gender in themselves, in others, and in the assessment and intervention instruments and techniques that they use, and how these biases can affect teaching, decisions, behavior, and long-term outcomes for students; and work to decrease such biases (b). They endorse and use practices that allow all children, regardless of their background, to feel welcomed and appreciated in the school and in the community (c). The interventions that they design and implement to effect learning and behavioral goals and objectives are informed by their understanding of students' backgrounds, cultural attributes, and individual learning styles and characteristics (d).

97. B: Informed consent does not include commitment to complete the experiment. When participants in experimental research sign written consents, they are not giving consent to finish the study. In fact, informed consent includes the provision that they can leave the study at any time (d) without being penalized in any way. Before signing, participants are to be informed of the procedures that will be used in the experiment(s), and also of the possible risks and benefits to them (a). They are assured that all records of their participation are kept private and confidential (c); these records may not be made public unless the participant gives approval. Participants are also to be given the names, phone numbers, and other contact information of officials they can contact if they wish to report any grievances (e) about the research or the way it was conducted.

98. C: It is false that school psychology uses educational psychology principles but not clinical psychology principles. School psychology's origins were concurrent with the origins of the field of psychology (a) itself, i.e. it began as early as the field of psychology did. It also has connections to both clinical psychology and functional psychology (b). Functionalism was opposed to structuralism and was founded by William James. Some scholars claim clinical psychologists want to know what occurs with children and how it occurs, while functional psychologists also want to know why; school psychologists take their orientations from both. School psychology began as a part of the social reform of the late 19th and early 20th centuries (d). School psychology resulted from compulsory education laws and the need for special education (e). When child labor laws were passed prohibiting minor children from working in factories, compulsory education laws were also passed. Both laws were due to the focus on children in social reform movements. Because of these laws, children with disabilities attended school. Educators realized these children needed alternative teaching methods. In the early 1900s a number of schools created small special education classrooms, and educators saw a need for experts to select children for special education. This need resulted in the birth of school psychology.

99. D: Lightner Witmer is founded the first psychological and child guidance clinic at the University of Pennsylvania in 1896, and advocated for children with special education needs. Witmer studied under both James McKeen Cattell (a), who helped establish psychology as a legitimate science, and Wilhelm Wundt (b), who is regarded as the father of experimental psychology. Arnold Gesell (c) a pediatrician and psychologist, was the first American school psychologist, and worked as such in Massachusetts. Gesell opened the Clinic of Child Development at Yale. G. Stanley Hall (e), a mentor to Gesell, was the first president of the American Psychological Association (APA), and founded the American Journal of Psychology in 1892. Hall is also remembered for his "storm and stress" theory of adolescence.

100. A: It is false that HIPAA is determined via individual states' laws. HIPAA is a Federal law. HIPAA stands for the Health Insurance Portability and Accountability Act. This 1996 law was sponsored by Senators Edward Kennedy (D-Massachusetts) and Nancy Kassebaum (R-Kansas). Title I of this law protects health insurance for employees and their families if they change or lose their jobs (e). HIPAA also dictates the standards for protecting the privacy of a client's or student's health records, including therapy records (d). Title II of this law mandates the creation of national standards for electronic health care transactions and national identifiers for health insurance plans, providers, and employers. It regulates the electronic transmission of student/client records (b) as well as information used in health insurance claims (c).

How to Overcome Test Anxiety

Just the thought of taking a test is enough to make most people a little nervous. A test is an important event that can have a long-term impact on your future, so it's important to take it seriously and it's natural to feel anxious about performing well. But just because anxiety is normal, that doesn't mean that it's helpful in test taking, or that you should simply accept it as part of your life. Anxiety can have a variety of effects. These effects can be mild, like making you feel slightly nervous, or severe, like blocking your ability to focus or remember even a simple detail.

If you experience test anxiety—whether severe or mild—it's important to know how to beat it. To discover this, first you need to understand what causes test anxiety.

Causes of Test Anxiety

While we often think of anxiety as an uncontrollable emotional state, it can actually be caused by simple, practical things. One of the most common causes of test anxiety is that a person does not feel adequately prepared for their test. This feeling can be the result of many different issues such as poor study habits or lack of organization, but the most common culprit is time management. Starting to study too late, failing to organize your study time to cover all of the material, or being distracted while you study will mean that you're not well prepared for the test. This may lead to cramming the night before, which will cause you to be physically and mentally exhausted for the test. Poor time management also contributes to feelings of stress, fear, and hopelessness as you realize you are not well prepared but don't know what to do about it.

Other times, test anxiety is not related to your preparation for the test but comes from unresolved fear. This may be a past failure on a test, or poor performance on tests in general. It may come from comparing yourself to others who seem to be performing better or from the stress of living up to expectations. Anxiety may be driven by fears of the future—how failure on this test would affect your educational and career goals. These fears are often completely irrational, but they can still negatively impact your test performance.

Elements of Test Anxiety

As mentioned earlier, test anxiety is considered to be an emotional state, but it has physical and mental components as well. Sometimes you may not even realize that you are suffering from test anxiety until you notice the physical symptoms. These can include trembling hands, rapid heartbeat, sweating, nausea, and tense muscles. Extreme anxiety may lead to fainting or vomiting. Obviously, any of these symptoms can have a negative impact on testing. It is important to recognize them as soon as they begin to occur so that you can address the problem before it damages your performance.

The mental components of test anxiety include trouble focusing and inability to remember learned information. During a test, your mind is on high alert, which can help you recall information and stay focused for an extended period of time. However, anxiety interferes with your mind's natural processes, causing you to blank out, even on the questions you know well. The strain of testing during anxiety makes it difficult to stay focused, especially on a test that may take several hours. Extreme anxiety can take a huge mental toll, making it difficult not only to recall test information but even to understand the test questions or pull your thoughts together.

Effects of Test Anxiety

Test anxiety is like a disease—if left untreated, it will get progressively worse. Anxiety leads to poor performance, and this reinforces the feelings of fear and failure, which in turn lead to poor performances on subsequent tests. It can grow from a mild nervousness to a crippling condition. If allowed to progress, test anxiety can have a big impact on your schooling, and consequently on your future.

Test anxiety can spread to other parts of your life. Anxiety on tests can become anxiety in any stressful situation, and blanking on a test can turn into panicking in a job situation. But fortunately, you don't have to let anxiety rule your testing and determine your grades. There are a number of relatively simple steps you can take to move past anxiety and function normally on a test and in the rest of life.

Physical Steps for Beating Test Anxiety

While test anxiety is a serious problem, the good news is that it can be overcome. It doesn't have to control your ability to think and remember information. While it may take time, you can begin taking steps today to beat anxiety.

Just as your first hint that you may be struggling with anxiety comes from the physical symptoms, the first step to treating it is also physical. Rest is crucial for having a clear, strong mind. If you are tired, it is much easier to give in to anxiety. But if you establish good sleep habits, your body and mind will be ready to perform optimally, without the strain of exhaustion. Additionally, sleeping well helps you to retain information better, so you're more likely to recall the answers when you see the test questions.

Getting good sleep means more than going to bed on time. It's important to allow your brain time to relax. Take study breaks from time to time so it doesn't get overworked, and don't study right before bed. Take time to rest your mind before trying to rest your body, or you may find it difficult to fall asleep.

Along with sleep, other aspects of physical health are important in preparing for a test. Good nutrition is vital for good brain function. Sugary foods and drinks may give a burst of energy but this burst is followed by a crash, both physically and emotionally. Instead, fuel your body with protein and vitamin-rich foods.

Also, drink plenty of water. Dehydration can lead to headaches and exhaustion, especially if your brain is already under stress from the rigors of the test. Particularly if your test is a long one, drink water during the breaks. And if possible, take an energy-boosting snack to eat between sections.

Along with sleep and diet, a third important part of physical health is exercise. Maintaining a steady workout schedule is helpful, but even taking 5-minute study breaks to walk can help get your blood pumping faster and clear your head. Exercise also releases endorphins, which contribute to a positive feeling and can help combat test anxiety.

When you nurture your physical health, you are also contributing to your mental health. If your body is healthy, your mind is much more likely to be healthy as well. So take time to rest, nourish your body with healthy food and water, and get moving as much as possible. Taking these physical steps will make you stronger and more able to take the mental steps necessary to overcome test anxiety.

Mental Steps for Beating Test Anxiety

Working on the mental side of test anxiety can be more challenging, but as with the physical side, there are clear steps you can take to overcome it. As mentioned earlier, test anxiety often stems from lack of preparation, so the obvious solution is to prepare for the test. Effective studying may be the most important weapon you have for beating test anxiety, but you can and should employ several other mental tools to combat fear.

First, boost your confidence by reminding yourself of past success—tests or projects that you aced. If you're putting as much effort into preparing for this test as you did for those, there's no reason you should expect to fail here. Work hard to prepare; then trust your preparation.

Second, surround yourself with encouraging people. It can be helpful to find a study group, but be sure that the people you're around will encourage a positive attitude. If you spend time with others who are anxious or cynical, this will only contribute to your own anxiety. Look for others who are motivated to study hard from a desire to succeed, not from a fear of failure.

Third, reward yourself. A test is physically and mentally tiring, even without anxiety, and it can be helpful to have something to look forward to. Plan an activity following the test, regardless of the outcome, such as going to a movie or getting ice cream.

When you are taking the test, if you find yourself beginning to feel anxious, remind yourself that you know the material. Visualize successfully completing the test. Then take a few deep, relaxing breaths and return to it. Work through the questions carefully but with confidence, knowing that you are capable of succeeding.

Developing a healthy mental approach to test taking will also aid in other areas of life. Test anxiety affects more than just the actual test—it can be damaging to your mental health and even contribute to depression. It's important to beat test anxiety before it becomes a problem for more than testing.

Study Strategy

Being prepared for the test is necessary to combat anxiety, but what does being prepared look like? You may study for hours on end and still not feel prepared. What you need is a strategy for test prep. The next few pages outline our recommended steps to help you plan out and conquer the challenge of preparation.

Step 1: Scope Out the Test

Learn everything you can about the format (multiple choice, essay, etc.) and what will be on the test. Gather any study materials, course outlines, or sample exams that may be available. Not only will this help you to prepare, but knowing what to expect can help to alleviate test anxiety.

Step 2: Map Out the Material

Look through the textbook or study guide and make note of how many chapters or sections it has. Then divide these over the time you have. For example, if a book has 15 chapters and you have five days to study, you need to cover three chapters each day. Even better, if you have the time, leave an extra day at the end for overall review after you have gone through the material in depth.

If time is limited, you may need to prioritize the material. Look through it and make note of which sections you think you already have a good grasp on, and which need review. While you are studying, skim quickly through the familiar sections and take more time on the challenging parts.

Write out your plan so you don't get lost as you go. Having a written plan also helps you feel more in control of the study, so anxiety is less likely to arise from feeling overwhelmed at the amount to cover.

Step 3: Gather Your Tools

Decide what study method works best for you. Do you prefer to highlight in the book as you study and then go back over the highlighted portions? Or do you type out notes of the important information? Or is it helpful to make flashcards that you can carry with you? Assemble the pens, index cards, highlighters, post-it notes, and any other materials you may need so you won't be distracted by getting up to find things while you study.

If you're having a hard time retaining the information or organizing your notes, experiment with different methods. For example, try color-coding by subject with colored pens, highlighters, or post-it notes. If you learn better by hearing, try recording yourself reading your notes so you can listen while in the car, working out, or simply sitting at your desk. Ask a friend to quiz you from your flashcards, or try teaching someone the material to solidify it in your mind.

Step 4: Create Your Environment

It's important to avoid distractions while you study. This includes both the obvious distractions like visitors and the subtle distractions like an uncomfortable chair (or a too-comfortable couch that makes you want to fall asleep). Set up the best study environment possible: good lighting and a comfortable work area. If background music helps you focus, you may want to turn it on, but otherwise keep the room quiet. If you are using a computer to take notes, be sure you don't have any other windows open, especially applications like social media, games, or anything else that could distract you. Silence your phone and turn off notifications. Be sure to keep water close by so you stay hydrated while you study (but avoid unhealthy drinks and snacks).

Also, take into account the best time of day to study. Are you freshest first thing in the morning? Try to set aside some time then to work through the material. Is your mind clearer in the afternoon or evening? Schedule your study session then. Another method is to study at the same time of day that you will take the test, so that your brain gets used to working on the material at that time and will be ready to focus at test time.

Step 5: Study!

Once you have done all the study preparation, it's time to settle into the actual studying. Sit down, take a few moments to settle your mind so you can focus, and begin to follow your study plan. Don't give in to distractions or let yourself procrastinate. This is your time to prepare so you'll be ready to fearlessly approach the test. Make the most of the time and stay focused.

Of course, you don't want to burn out. If you study too long you may find that you're not retaining the information very well. Take regular study breaks. For example, taking five minutes out of every hour to walk briskly, breathing deeply and swinging your arms, can help your mind stay fresh.

As you get to the end of each chapter or section, it's a good idea to do a quick review. Remind yourself of what you learned and work on any difficult parts. When you feel that you've mastered the material, move on to the next part. At the end of your study session, briefly skim through your notes again.

But while review is helpful, cramming last minute is NOT. If at all possible, work ahead so that you won't need to fit all your study into the last day. Cramming overloads your brain with more information than it can process and retain, and your tired mind may struggle to recall even previously learned information when it is overwhelmed with last-minute study. Also, the urgent nature of cramming and the stress placed on your brain contribute to anxiety. You'll be more likely to go to the test feeling unprepared and having trouble thinking clearly.

So don't cram, and don't stay up late before the test, even just to review your notes at a leisurely pace. Your brain needs rest more than it needs to go over the information again. In fact, plan to finish your studies by noon or early afternoon the day before the test. Give your brain the rest of the day to relax or focus on other things, and get a good night's sleep. Then you will be fresh for the test and better able to recall what you've studied.

Step 6: Take a Practice Test

Many courses offer sample tests, either online or in the study materials. This is an excellent resource to check whether you have mastered the material, as well as to prepare for the test format and environment.

Check the test format ahead of time: the number of questions, the type (multiple choice, free response, etc.), and the time limit. Then create a plan for working through them. For example, if you have 30 minutes to take a 60-question test, your limit is 30 seconds per question. Spend less time on the questions you know well so that you can take more time on the difficult ones.

If you have time to take several practice tests, take the first one open book, with no time limit. Work through the questions at your own pace and make sure you fully understand them. Gradually work up to taking a test under test conditions: sit at a desk with all study materials put away and set a timer. Pace yourself to make sure you finish the test with time to spare and go back to check your answers if you have time.

After each test, check your answers. On the questions you missed, be sure you understand why you missed them. Did you misread the question (tests can use tricky wording)? Did you forget the information? Or was it something you hadn't learned? Go back and study any shaky areas that the practice tests reveal.

Taking these tests not only helps with your grade, but also aids in combating test anxiety. If you're already used to the test conditions, you're less likely to worry about it, and working through tests until you're scoring well gives you a confidence boost. Go through the practice tests until you feel comfortable, and then you can go into the test knowing that you're ready for it.

Test Tips

On test day, you should be confident, knowing that you've prepared well and are ready to answer the questions. But aside from preparation, there are several test day strategies you can employ to maximize your performance.

First, as stated before, get a good night's sleep the night before the test (and for several nights before that, if possible). Go into the test with a fresh, alert mind rather than staying up late to study.

Try not to change too much about your normal routine on the day of the test. It's important to eat a nutritious breakfast, but if you normally don't eat breakfast at all, consider eating just a protein bar. If you're a coffee drinker, go ahead and have your normal coffee. Just make sure you time it so that the caffeine doesn't wear off right in the middle of your test. Avoid sugary beverages, and drink enough water to stay hydrated but not so much that you need a restroom break 10 minutes into the test. If your test isn't first thing in the morning, consider going for a walk or doing a light workout before the test to get your blood flowing.

Allow yourself enough time to get ready, and leave for the test with plenty of time to spare so you won't have the anxiety of scrambling to arrive in time. Another reason to be early is to select a good seat. It's helpful to sit away from doors and windows, which can be distracting. Find a good seat, get out your supplies, and settle your mind before the test begins.

When the test begins, start by going over the instructions carefully, even if you already know what to expect. Make sure you avoid any careless mistakes by following the directions.

Then begin working through the questions, pacing yourself as you've practiced. If you're not sure on an answer, don't spend too much time on it, and don't let it shake your confidence. Either skip it and come back later, or eliminate as many wrong answers as possible and guess among the remaining ones. Don't dwell on these questions as you continue—put them out of your mind and focus on what lies ahead.

Be sure to read all of the answer choices, even if you're sure the first one is the right answer. Sometimes you'll find a better one if you keep reading. But don't second-guess yourself if you do immediately know the answer. Your gut instinct is usually right. Don't let test anxiety rob you of the information you know.

If you have time at the end of the test (and if the test format allows), go back and review your answers. Be cautious about changing any, since your first instinct tends to be correct, but make sure you didn't misread any of the questions or accidentally mark the wrong answer choice. Look over any you skipped and make an educated guess.

At the end, leave the test feeling confident. You've done your best, so don't waste time worrying about your performance or wishing you could change anything. Instead, celebrate the successful completion of this test. And finally, use this test to learn how to deal with anxiety even better next time.

Review Video: Test Anxiety
Visit mometrix.com/academy and enter code: 100340

Important Qualification

Not all anxiety is created equal. If your test anxiety is causing major issues in your life beyond the classroom or testing center, or if you are experiencing troubling physical symptoms related to your anxiety, it may be a sign of a serious physiological or psychological condition. If this sounds like your situation, we strongly encourage you to seek professional help.

Online Resources

Due to our efforts to try to keep this book to a manageable length, we've created a link that will give you access to all of your online resources:

mometrix.com/resources719/clepintedpsy

It's Your Moment, Let's Celebrate It!

Share your story @mometrixtestpreparation